*UFOs:*
*FRIEND, FOE*
*OR FANTASY?*

# UFOs

## Friend, Foe or Fantasy?

### A BIBLICAL PERSPECTIVE ON THE PHENOMENON OF THE CENTURY

William R. Goetz

## HORIZON BOOKs

CAMP HILL, PENNSYLVANIA

Horizon Books
3825 Hartzdale Drive, Camp Hill, PA 17011
www.cpi-horizon.com

ISBN: 0-88965-141-8

97  98  99  00  01      5  4  3  2  1

*Sincere thanks to . . .*

. . . my wife Joyce who patiently put up with the disruption of our normal family life while this volume was being written;

. . . the friends of the New Buffalo, Pennsylvania, Alliance Church, and especially Dale Simmons, who provided me with a computer and expertise;

. . . David Fessenden, my patient, skillful editor;

. . . Hank Hanegraaff, of Christian Research Institute, who graciously permitted the use of the title of one of the late Dr. Walter Martin's CRI booklets and cassettes as the title of this book and

. . . a number of friends, too numerous to mention by name, who kindly provided prayer support and research materials during this endeavor.

*To all these, this volume is affectionately dedicated.*

# CONTENTS

# INTRODUCTION

## *How This Book Came to Be Written and Why It Is Different*

In a word—it was an assignment from the Editorial Board of Christian Publications/Horizon Books, of which I am chairman.

Why me?

Until this assignment I'd not been intensely, compellingly interested in UFOs. I had researched the subject and briefly touched on it in my two previous books, *Apocalypse Next* and *The Economy to Come*. But I was certainly no authority. So why was I asked to do this project?

Here's how it happened.

In August 1996, our board's wide-ranging discussions of potential new titles included the subject of UFOs. Over the course of several meetings as that possibility was explored, I recalled aloud that I had written several articles on UFOs for *Compass* magazine back in the early 1960s, had interviewed the late Dr. Walter Martin on the subject and knew personally five colleagues or friends who had seen UFOs. I recounted the fact that I had also done UFO research in a minor way in connection with my previous books. In addition, I expressed the view, put forward in those books, that the increasing appearances of UFOs and the growing interest in them had prophetic significance.

My voicing of these observations was not an attempt to obtain a book assignment. Rather it was done simply to help us decide, as a board, if we should assign a UFO title.

As you know, since you're reading this book, the decision was to publish. I was assigned.

Since the assignment I have, for the greater part of a year, "breathed, slept, eaten and dreamt" UFOs and ufology. I've researched scores of books, newspapers, magazines, journals and research papers. The internet, with its plethora of UFO information, has been perused. I've viewed dozens of videos, films and TV programs; I've listened to numerous recorded lectures, being careful in all of the above to research what both believers and skeptics have said or are saying. On various occasions I found myself behaving like a detective, tracking down one lead after another.

During several periods, especially as the deadline neared, virtually every waking hour apart from my normal responsibilities was devoted to research and writing. A week and a half of vacation time was gobbled up by the project at that point.

Then, as the end was in sight, news of the tragic mass suicide of thirty-nine members of the

Heaven's Gate UFO cult grabbed the spotlight in the national media and held it for days. The cultists believed that after death a spacecraft would take them to "the next level of existence." While it fit completely into the thesis of this book, it added a major and tragic dimension.

In the process of this writing my mind has been boggled by the magnitude and pervasiveness of the phenomena. And I'm amazed at the widespread interest in the possibility that UFOs are the vehicles of extraterrestrials (ETs) who are coming with a message for mankind.

To be sure, that interest is divided into two basic groups: believers and skeptics (including "debunkers"). But regardless of the perspective, the interest is intense. And the fascination with the subject has been growing. It is fueled by an expanding number of books, magazines, newsletters, internet web pages, newspaper articles and TV programs, as well as UFO conferences and seminars. Whitley Strieber's UFO books *Communion*, *Transformation* and *Breakthrough* have spent months on the best-seller lists. Movies, videos and TV programs such as *Star Trek*; *Close Encounters of the Third Kind*; *2001: A Space Odyssey*; *Dark Skies*; *Alien Autopsy*; *Roswell: The UFO Cover-Up*; *The X-Files*; *Sightings* and more have impacted millions.

Then in mid-1996 the movie *Independence Day* exploded on the scene. This dramatic portrayal of an alien invasion of earth has incredible special effects, but a story line that is frequently *completely* absurd and unbelievable. Nevertheless it had an awesome response. *TIME* magazine called it "the No. 1 film of the year"; *Newsweek*, *USA Today* and the *Boston Globe* all dubbed it a "blockbuster." Most theaters were sold out; even those which ran the feature around the clock drew full houses. The film broke all previous box office records.

The popularity of this genre of movies and TV programs has spawned a growing number of similar releases: the TV series *Millennium* premiered in the fall of '96; *Mars Attacks* (a spoof on the alien invasion theme, but still an indicator of popular interest) came out that Christmas; the UFO-related comedy *Men in Black* and the drama *Contact* were among the biggest films of summer 1997. And the producers of *Independence Day* have a sequel or two in the works—to name but a few.

The week of June 16-21, 1997 was a big one for UFO emphasis in America. First, *TIME* did a cover story on the fiftieth anniversary of an alleged crash-landing of a flying saucer in Roswell, New Mexico. Then throughout the week *USA Today* and the major TV networks ran stories and features on the March 13, 1997 sightings of strange lights over Arizona. The event had been videotaped and was shown on network television. Hundreds of people from Tucson in the south to Kingman in the northwest of Arizona had called authorities and the Seattle-based National UFO Reporting Center about the as-yet-unexplained sightings.

The fiftieth anniversary of the Roswell crash saw celebrations from July 1-6 in that New Mexico city of 48,000, which drew over 20,000 UFO buffs to the event. The celebration created enormous renewed worldwide interest in the UFO phenomenon.

A significant prelude to the anniversary was the June 1997 release of a USAF publication entitled *The Roswell Report: Case Closed.* The book was described by the Air Force as the "final explanation" of what really happened in Roswell in 1947. In actual fact, rather than closing the book on long-standing rumors, the detailed explanation that the dead "aliens" were crash dummies used in parachute tests simply added fuel to the debate over the alleged official cover-up of a flying saucer crash and recovery of extraterrestrial bodies.

I believe that all of this steadily increasing fascination with alien intelligence and their purported interaction with earth is part of a major massaging of humanity concerning the paranormal. Thus I am more convinced than ever that the UFO phenomenon has prophetic significance. I am also certain that the Bible does speak to the issue. Not specifically, but very clearly on principle.

Consequently I believe that, far from being a topic suitable only for kooks, ufologists and New Agers, a consideration of UFOs is of vital spiritual importance to everyone.

I propose to show that many of the UFO encounters reported in both ancient and modern times have been real experiences. But I submit that rather than involving extraterrestrials, they have a different origin. Through a careful consid-

eration of the symptoms evidenced by many "abductees" and the messages resulting from these
encounters, the true nature of this phenomenon
will be detailed.

The Word of God, particularly in its prophetic
aspect, will then be applied to these conclusions,
providing what I believe is the divine perspective
on this vitally important subject.

It has major implications for every one of us!

# Part One

# Fantasy
## or
# Reality?

In the past fifty years there have been claims of literally millions of UFO sightings around the world.

Are they real?

Approximately half of Americans, according to periodic polls, believe they are![1] And this percentage has remained fairly constant for the past twenty years.[2] The belief has produced what amounts to a genuine UFO subculture.

But among the other half—the skeptics who are either not sure, or who do *not* believe—are the debunkers. They've been led by, among others, Philip Klass, the late

Carl Sagan and The Committee for the Scientific Investigation of Claims of the Paranormal—publishers of the respected periodical *The Skeptical Inquirer*. This group claims that the UFO experiences are all entirely fantasy.

Who's right?

Let's investigate.

# CHAPTER ONE

# *The Claims Are Impressive*

It was less than an hour after the evening service concluded at Sevenoaks Alliance Church in Abbotsford, British Columbia on May 3, 1978. Suddenly, Sean Campbell and Mike Nyvall, two young men just back from their freshman year at college, rushed in excitedly. They had just seen what they believed was a UFO and had come directly from the police station where they had gone to report it.

Sean and Mike had been about to cross the Trans-Canada Highway on an overpass just west of the city when the incident occurred. Sean recalls:

Mike was driving and I looked up and saw peculiar lights. They couldn't have been more than a couple thousand feet up. At first I thought I was simply seeing some reflection and tried to screen it out. But I couldn't. Whatever it was, it had white

11

lights and appeared to be spinning. Mike immediately looked up, and I realized he was seeing the same thing. We drove right up to the overpass, got out and, from the overpass, watched "the thing" proceed almost directly over the highway, heading west. We could see it clearly and watched it till it went out of sight. It definitely wasn't a plane or a helicopter. It didn't move fast at all.

From there we drove to the Matsqui police station—somewhat reluctantly, because we could hardly believe it ourselves. We apologized to one of the officers there for sounding ridiculous and told him what we had seen. Nothing had been reported to the police at that point, but the officer was kind, listened and took notes. After we finished he said, "Guys, I thought I saw a UFO once, too. I think they're real."

Mike and I felt that certainly other people must have seen it too and we watched the papers, but heard nothing more about it. (Personal fax, December 5, 1996)

The incident made a strong impression on the young men. When I recently phoned Sean, now the Canadian director of Franklin Graham's Samaritan's Purse relief agency, he immediately and vividly recalled the sighting, though almost two decades have passed since it occurred.

## A Ministerial Sighting

Some eighteen months after that event I learned that three pastoral colleagues—Rev. Mel and Mrs. Jean Shareski and Rev. Graham Clark—had sighted a UFO on their way from Vancouver, British Columbia to Red Deer, Alberta to attend a prayer retreat.

Mel and Jean have since both passed away, but a conversation in early 1997 with Pastor Clark, now retired, revealed that the sighting had a profound effect upon him. Though nearly eighteen years had passed, Graham recalled it vividly and in detail.

The sighting occurred at early evening in mid-September, shortly after darkness had fallen. Mel was driving, with Jean beside him in the front seat. Graham was tired and reclining in the back seat, since they had driven most of the day from Vancouver. They were passing through the foothills of the Canadian Rockies in a part of the province that, even today, is very sparsely populated; only a couple of small towns are located in the entire seventy-five-mile section between Banff and Calgary, Alberta. The nearest major airport is at least fifty miles away.

Suddenly Graham became aware of a nearby light in the sky, visible through the side window. It came from a reddish-orange object, circular in shape, which looked like a "flying ring" and seemed to be just floating in the air. The object appeared to be about half a mile from the car and

200-300 feet above the ground. It did not look or behave like a conventional plane or helicopter as it kept pace, exactly, with their car.

Graham brought the object to the attention of Mel and Jean. The trio was mystified as to what it might be. They discussed a variety of possibilities as the object accompanied them for over half an hour while they covered about twenty-five miles of highway. They agreed that they had "an eerie feeling" about the light—as though they were "being watched" even while they were watching it. Graham personally felt an oppressive spirit.

Then, as suddenly as it had appeared, it was gone.

At the conference the three told a number of people, myself included, about their unusual experience, which seemed to be the end of it. However, it had a profound effect, for, as indicated earlier, nearly eighteen years later Graham not only vividly remembered, but felt a sense of relief—relief that I was inquiring in all seriousness. He said he had often felt "alone and almost kooky" concerning what he and the Shareskis had witnessed (telephone conversation, January 6, 1997).

The experiences of my friends were but two comparatively unspectacular "Close Encounters of the First Kind" (CE1) among what is believed to be millions of such occurrences worldwide in the past fifty years.

But the modern era of UFO sightings, which began in 1947, is merely the current wave of similar events that have had a lengthy history.

## UFOs in History

Dr. Jacques Vallee, an astrophysicist who is regarded as the world's foremost researcher of and authority on UFOs, writes that contemporary reports of UFO encounters "are consistent with perplexing accounts that come to us from earlier times, from the oldest records we have."[1]

Vallee then lists some of these accounts. As do many other writers, he suggests that the biblical records of the burning bush, the pillar of cloud and fire, the whirlwind, Ezekiel's "wheel in a wheel" and so on, are descriptions of UFO encounters. While I disagree (and I will explain why later), it is a widely held view.

The Joman Era of ancient Japan, ending around 3000 B.C., has left artifacts which closely resemble the current understanding of extraterrestrials' appearance.[2] An account from the year 1180 A.D. describes a luminous flying object like an "earthenware vessel" sighted in Japan's *Kii* province. It has been suggested that this is truly the first "flying saucer." Other mysterious flying objects are reported in Japanese records in the years 989, 1235, 1271, 1361, 1458, 1569, 1702 and 1749.[3]

W. Raymond Drake in his *Gods and Spacemen in the Ancient East* combines recent scientific discoveries with archeological evidence to show how the records of a number of ancient civilizations contain descriptions of mysterious entities from "the heavens"—obviously space, in the author's view. Drake explores the histories of ancient India, Tibet, China, Egypt and Babylon, among others, and shows how their "heavenly" visitors correspond to our present-day UFOs.[4]

*We Are Not the First*, by Andrew Tomas, contains a description of numerous stone carvings and engravings from past civilizations which depict beings that, in their attire and vehicles, appear to be what we know of space travelers today. Tomas reviews classic writings such as the Indian *Ramayana* which describe aerial "chariots"—some circular or double-decker with portholes and domes, and the capacity to fly with "the speed of the wind."[5]

Christopher Columbus apparently sighted a UFO. In the September 15, 1492 entry in his ship's log he described a "marvelous branch of fire [which] fell from the heavens into the sea." It then exited from the water and returned to the skies. Columbus would surely have known about the phenomenon of falling stars, so the incident must have been something out of the ordinary to cause him to describe it as "marvelous."[6]

Pierre Boaistuau, a sixteenth-century writer, described an occurrence at Tubingen, Germany, on December 5, 1577 at 7 a.m.:

> About the sun many dark clouds appeared, such as we are wont to see during great storms: and soon afterward have come from the sun other clouds, all fiery and bloody, and others, yellow as saffron. Out of these clouds have come forth reverberations resembling large, tall and wide hats, and the

earth showed itself yellow and bloody, and seemed to be covered with hats, tall and wide, which appeared in various colors such as red, blue, green and most of them black.[7]

Anyone who has done any UFO research at all readily recognizes the link between the objects reported by Boaistuau and reports of modern-day UFO characteristics.

The English astronomer Edmund Halley, discoverer of the comet named after him, was sent a UFO report by an Italian professor of mathematics. He reported seeing, in March of 1676, a "vast body apparently bigger than the moon," which crossed over all Italy. It was at an estimated height of forty miles, made a hissing sound and a noise "like the rattling of a great cart over stones." The professor calculated its speed at 160 miles a minute—9,600 miles an hour. Halley's comment was: "I find it one of the hardest things to account for that I have ever met." However, the next year, in 1677, Halley himself reported observing "a great light in the sky all over southern England, many miles high."[8]

Closer to our time, there was a wave of sightings of a mysterious "flying machine" over many parts of the United States in the late 1890s. It began in San Francisco in 1896 when startled residents spotted a large, elongated dark object in the sky. It carried brilliant searchlights and was able to fly against the wind. Later, beginning in April 1897, what appeared to be the same object made

an astonishing number of appearances in the Mid-
west, often traveling slowly and majestically over
large urban areas like Omaha, Milwaukee and
Chicago, where great crowds gathered to watch
the spectacle. Newspapers were full of the accounts of the phenomenon.

At times the airship, which predated the
Wright brothers' invention of the heavier-than-
air plane by several years, abandoned its stately
pace and darted about like a modern UFO,
changing course and altitude abruptly, swooping
at impossible speeds, circling, landing, taking off
or sweeping the countryside with powerful
beams of light. It also made mechanical noises,
like the clanking and rumbling of engines or the
whooshes made by compressed air. Several
claims were made by various individuals of approaches to the landed vessel and encounters
with some of its occupants.[9]

Today, as they were at the time, researchers are
divided concerning these events. Some attribute
the sightings to deliberate hoaxes and contagious
rumors. Others argue that at least some of these
aerial events originated from "the same mysterious source beyond time and space" from which
their eventual descendants, the flying saucers,
come.[10]

Vallee accepts the accounts as authentic and
writes that:

> the rediscovery of the remarkable wave of
> reports [the airship] generated has provided

a crucial missing link between the apparitions of older days and modern saucer stories, thanks to researchers such as Donald Hanlon, Jerome Clark, and Lucius Farish.[11]

And he believes that there have been many such UFO events throughout history. In his book *Passport to Magonia*, Vallee provides a carefully researched catalog of over 900 UFO-type sightings or encounters in the century from 1868 to 1968![12]

## UFOs in Modern Times

The current era of UFO sightings began about fifty years after the airship flap.

An Associated Press dispatch on June 25, 1947 introduced the modern wave of UFO sightings. Originating in Pendleton, Oregon, the wire story captured the attention of the nation with the following account:

> Nine bright saucer-like objects flying at "incredible speed" at 10,000 feet altitude were reported here today by Kenneth Arnold, Boise, Idaho, pilot who said he could not hazard a guess as to what they were.
>
> Arnold, a United States Forest Service employee engaged in searching for a missing plane, said he sighted the mysterious objects yesterday at 3 p.m. They were flying between Mount Rainier and Mount Adams, in Washington State, he said, and appeared to wave in and out of formation. Arnold said he

clocked and estimated their speed at 1,200 miles an hour.

Inquiries at Yakima last night brought only blank stares, he said, but he added he talked with an unidentified man from Utah, south of here, who said he had seen similar objects over the mountains near Ukiah yesterday.

"It seems impossible," Arnold said, "but there it is."[13]

Because Arnold—a rescue pilot, businessman and deputy sheriff—was a well-regarded citizen, the small group of journalists who had gotten wind of the event suspended their initial skepticism and reported the incident as a serious news story. The term "flying saucer" entered the nation's vocabulary as a result, and the UFO era of the twentieth century was launched.

In the resulting furor, which saw many people come forward with their own accounts of UFO sightings—some of which proved to be hoaxes— Arnold came to be perceived as "practically a moron." Fed up with the attention and ridicule, Arnold said later, "If I saw a ten-story building flying through the air I wouldn't say a word about it. Half the people I see look at me as a combination of Einstein, Flash Gordon and Screwball."[14]

## It Actually Began Years Before

To be strictly factual, the current UFO wave began earlier than 1947.

In the summer of 1906, as a British steamer plowed its way through the Persian Gulf near Oman, an enormous wheel of light appeared in the sky. The huge object, seemingly bigger than the ship itself, was revolving not far above the surface of the water. Vivid shafts of light were emitted by the giant wheel, some of which passed through the steamer itself—without harm. Witnesses remarked on the "eerie silence" of the phenomenon. The Gulf sighting was one of eleven such recorded reports of mysterious wheel appearances between 1848 and 1910.[15]

Later, from 1946 to 1948, witnesses in Sweden and Finland reported seeing strange, cigar-shaped objects flying close to the Soviet border. Such reports led U.S. Army intelligence agents to fear that these "ghost rockets," as they were called, might be Soviet secret weapons developed in collaboration with German scientists.[16] Fully twenty percent of these sightings had no explanation whatever.

The numerous reports by World War II pilots of "foo fighters"—mysterious balls of fire which played on or around their aircraft—are widely known. Disk-like objects following military planes were also frequently reported. No satisfactory explanation for these phenomena has ever been given, and so they remain UFOs.

A major event, which at first glance may not appear to be related to the UFO phenomenon, occurred in 1917 near the small Portuguese town of Fatima. And yet the famous apparitions of an en-

tity thought to be the Virgin Mary do relate, I believe, to UFOs.

Vallee certainly thinks so. In *Dimensions* he
writes:

> The [Virgin Mary apparitions] at Fatima
> involved luminous spheres, lights with
> strange colors, a feeling of "heat waves"—all
> physical characteristics commonly associ-
> ated with UFOs. They even included the
> typical falling-leaf motion of the saucer zig-
> zagging through the air. They also encom-
> passed prophecy and a loss of ordinary
> consciousness on the part of witnesses—
> what we have called the psychic component
> of UFO sightings.[17]

## An Amazing Six Months

The first apparition at Fatima took place on
May 13, 1917. Three children tending sheep were
surprised by a bright flash. Going to see what it
was, they were caught in a glowing light which almost blinded them. In the center of the light they
saw a little woman who begged them to return
every month to the same spot.

On June 13 fifty people accompanied the little
shepherds, who knelt transfixed, as if taken into
another world. The oldest child, a girl of ten,
spoke to an unseen entity whose answers were not
heard by the group. At the end of the one-sided
conversation all the witnesses heard an explosion

and saw a small cloud rise from near a tree, which became the center of all succeeding manifestations.

July 13 saw 4,500 witnesses gather. Detailed descriptions of physical phenomena consistent with UFO data were later made by many. The children received specific prophecies, some of which proved to be accurate, such as the outbreak of a war worse than World War I during the reign of Pius XI (World War II). A miracle was predicted for October 13.

On subsequent months the size of the crowd grew to 18,000, then 30,000 and finally 70,000 in October. Globes of light, shiny white "petals" or "angel's hair," flashes of light and a strange sweet fragrance were part of these apparitions.

At the final one on October 13 a heavy rain which had been falling suddenly stopped, the clouds parted and the sun appeared as a flat silver disk which spun rapidly and threw beams of colored lights in all directions. The disk then plunged downward in a zigzag manner toward the frightened spectators, most of whom began publicly praying in panicky confession of sin, convinced their end had come. Suddenly the disk reversed itself and disappeared into the real sun. The crowd realized, in astonishment, that their clothes were dry. The promised miracle had apparently occurred.

Subsequently numerous claims of miraculous healings were made by people who had witnessed the final "miracle" event.

In 1930, after thirteen years of intense investigation, the Catholic Church concluded that Fatima was a phenomenon, "witnessed by persons of all categories and social classes, believers and unbelievers, journalists and even persons some miles away," which could not be explained either as a physical effect or an illusion.

Vallee concludes that the apparitions "encompass all the physical characteristics commonly associated with UFOs," as well as the psychic components of such sightings.[18]

Associating Fatima or other Marian apparitions with UFOs (as a number of writers do) is a controversial conclusion.

Controversy also surrounds the multitude number of incidents which became public following the 1947 Arnold saucer sighting. Many are believed to be bona fide UFO encounters—unless one happens to be a debunker or a skeptic! Literally millions of sightings have gone on record.

For those who have done even a limited amount of research on the subject, the following overview of major UFO encounters since 1947 will appear woefully incomplete. For the uninitiated it may appear to be overkill! In actual fact it merely hits the high spots. There have been *millions* of reported UFO sightings from all over the globe in the past five decades.

## The Extraterrestrials Are Coming!

Less than two weeks after Kenneth Arnold's saucer sighting, one of the major UFO events of the century occurred. The Roswell, New Mexico, *Daily Record* headlined it on July 8, 1947:

### RAAF CAPTURES FLYING SAUCER
### IN ROSWELL REGION

The many rumors regarding the flying disc became a reality yesterday when the intelligence office of the 509th Bomb Group of the Eighth Air Force, Roswell Army Air Field, was fortunate enough to gain possession of a disc through the co-operation of one of the local ranchers and the Sheriff's office of Chaves County.[19]

The Associated Press picked up the story and the sensation was on. The amazing tale unfolded in the following fashion.

Sometime around 11:30 p.m. on Friday, the fourth of July, during a severe thunder and lightning storm, a number of individuals in and around the town of Roswell saw a brilliant blue-white light plunge to earth north of the town. James Ragsdale and Trudy Truelove, a couple who were camping in the desert, witnessed the object slam into the earth about a mile from their camp. They drove to the site and by means of a weak flashlight saw the remains of a vehicle. However, since there seemed to be nothing they could do, they decided to investigate further in the morning and went back to their camp.

The next day the couple returned to the crash site. In the daylight they saw what they thought was an experimental craft, crumpled against a small cliff. Near the wreckage Ragsdale observed several small bodies, but while he wanted to investigate further, Truelove, who was frightened, wanted to leave.

While they debated they heard a siren which heralded the arrival of a number of military vehicles, including a wrecker. Driving to a place of concealment in a nearby copse of trees and bushes, the pair watched as a tight cordon of vehicles and men was placed around the impact area. Ragsdale then yielded to Truelove's urgent desire to leave and they returned to their campsite, from which they left the area.[20]

## The Air Force Arrives

What happened next, according to researchers such as Kevin D. Randle and Donald R. Schmitt (authors of *The Truth About the UFO Crash at Roswell*), was that the military took the crashed vehicle and the dead occupants, under tight security, to the Roswell Air Force Base. There appeared to be good reason for the security.

According to sworn testimony from personnel on site at the time, the military had tracked—for a period of four days from July 1 to 4—an unidentified object in flight over New Mexico, including over the highly restricted White Sands Proving Grounds, site of the first atomic bomb detonation in 1945. When three sites (White Sands, Roswell and Albuquerque) tracking the object on July 4 saw it disappear from the radar screens shortly before 11:30 p.m. on the fourth, they were able to pinpoint the approximate location of the assumed crash. A comprehensive search located the wreckage the next day.

Numerous reports suggested that by July 8 the material recovered by the Roswell officers and men had been taken to Wright-Patterson Field in Dayton, Ohio. Civilians who had any exposure to the secretive proceedings were severely warned by military personnel not to talk about the event.[21] And perhaps it would have died there, so far as the media was concerned, except for a related occurrence.

## Meanwhile, Back at the Ranch . . .

On July 5, a rancher named William "Mac" Brazel went out on horseback with a young neighbor boy, William Proctor, to ride the range in a remote area of his ranch near Corona, New Mexico. They were checking to see if there had been damage from an earthshaking explosion which Brazel and his family had heard during the terrible storm the night before.

According to researchers Randle and Schmitt, they found more than they bargained for.

In a field south of the ranch headquarters, Brazel later reported, they discovered a great many large pieces of unusual debris scattered over a wide area. Some of it was like canvas or parchment; other pieces were of an incredibly light metal. Odd symbols, which vaguely resembled Egyptian hieroglyphics, were found on some of

the debris. And, though the material was extremely light, Brazel said he was unable to cut it
with his knife or burn it with matches.

Gathering some of the smaller samples, Brazel
drove about twenty miles to the ranch of William's parents, Floyd and Loretta Proctor. They
were as puzzled by it as he, but declined his sug-
gestion that they come with him to see the debris
field, being too busy.

The next day Brazel reluctantly decided that
he would have to drive the seventy-five miles to
Roswell to report his find. It had been suggested
to him that he may have found wreckage from a
classified military experiment, or even that he
might be able to claim one of the various re-
wards which were being offered for proof that
"flying saucers" existed. More practically, he
wanted to fix responsibility for the cleanup of
his field.

So the rancher went into Roswell to see the
Chaves County sheriff, George A. Wilcox. The
sheriff suggested a call to the local air base. In
response to the call, Major Jesse A. Marcel, the
intelligence officer on duty, went to the sheriff's
office, questioned Brazel and decided he would
need to visit the ranch. He returned to the base
and then, accompanied by Captain Sheridan
Cavitt, a plainclothes counterintelligence officer,
followed Brazel to the ranch in a separate vehicle. Since it was growing dark by the time they
arrived, an investigation was put off until the
next morning.

## Field Inspection

Early on July 7 the officers inspected the debris field. Marcel later said that the wreckage was scattered over an area "maybe three-quarters of a mile long and a few hundred feet wide." The two spent most of the day examining the field and picking up pieces of debris. Both of their vehicles were filled with the material, which they described as being thin and foil-like but so strong that even a sledgehammer couldn't dent it. Nor would the parchment-like debris burn.

The following day First Lieutenant Walter Haut, the public information officer at the 509th Bomb Group, took the press release partially quoted above to KGFL, a Roswell radio station, as well as to the two newspapers in the town. And so the word was out: the army had captured a flying saucer on a ranch near Roswell. Subsequently, reports of the recovery of the bodies of several aliens, including one still alive, circulated. Hangar 18, where the wreckage and bodies were taken, entered the UFO folklore of the era.

The next morning the wire services carried a very different story. The military's explanation was that what had been mistaken for the wreckage of a UFO was in reality nothing more than the remains of a battered Army weather balloon. And civilians who had any involvement with the material brought to the Air Force Base or found on the ranch were reportedly warned not to talk about it. Brazel allegedly was held under guard for a period of eight days. Military personnel, the manager of KGFL and others later claimed they had been threatened by authorities in Washington, D.C. to keep quiet about the incident.[22]

## It Polarizes Folks

The question of whether or not a UFO actually crashed in New Mexico in 1947 is one which still intrigues people. In fact, as the town of Roswell celebrated the fiftieth anniversary of the event, in July 1997, the question proved to be as much alive as ever. Did the military and the government engage in a cover-up—one that continues fifty years later?

A 1996 Discovery Channel program, "The Roswell Incident," featured interviews with a great many of the Roswell civilians who were living in the area at the time, as well as military personnel involved during the incident. The program also included comments by Ray Santelli, a British film producer who released a film in 1995 which purports to show an autopsy on the dead aliens. Santelli was interviewed between segments of the old film.[23] The impression left with viewers is that the event at Roswell did occur, even though Santelli's film has been widely denounced as a fraud by numerous researchers.

In the years since 1947 there have been literally millions of sightings all around the world. Permit me to give you a quick overview in chapter 2 of some of the more dramatic.

# CHAPTER TWO

# The "Killer" Saucer
# and Other Strange Incidents

On January 7, 1948, a call came in to the control tower of the Godman Air Force Base at Fort Knox, Kentucky from the State Highway Patrol. The police reported that townspeople about eighty miles away had seen a strange aircraft in the sky. After checking their records, the Godman personnel informed the police that there were no flights in the area in question. Shortly after, however, the control tower also sighted on radar an object which they were unable to identify.

The object had been tracked for about an hour when three F-51 Mustang fighters on a training exercise arrived in the area. The base commander asked the flight leader, Captain Thomas F. Mantell, to investigate the UFO.

The captain sighted what he radioed was "a metallic object of tremendous size" and began to climb toward it as it started to ascend rapidly. At 2:45 p.m., though it was risky to go beyond 15,000 feet without oxygen, Mantell told the tower that he was going to climb higher in order to get closer to the strange craft. It was the last thing he would ever say to anyone. At 25,000 feet the radar lost sight of the UFO and moments later Mantell's plane dived, exploding in midair. The wreckage was found ninety miles away.

Sensational headlines appeared across the nation. The official explanation was that the captain had passed out from lack of oxygen while mistakenly pursuing the planet Venus, but such a response did not satisfy many and the Mantell incident entered UFO legend.[1]

## Nash-Fortenberry Sighting

July 14, 1952 was a clear night with unlimited visibility. A PanAmerican airliner, piloted by Captain William B. Nash and copilot William Fortenberry, was approaching Norfolk, Virginia en route to Miami from New York.

Shortly after 8 p.m. the two pilots simultaneously caught sight of a red glow in the sky and "almost immediately perceived six bright objects streaking toward us at tremendous speed."

> [T]hey had the fiery aspect of hot coals, but of much greater glow—perhaps twenty times more brilliant than city lights below. . . . [T]heir shape . . . was evidently circular. . . . The objects, which were double the size of a

DC3, suddenly slowed, then all together
flipped on edge. . . . [T]hen, without an arc or
swerve at all, they flipped back together to the
flat altitude [sic] and darted off in a direction
that formed a sharp angle to their first course.
. . . [T]he change . . . was acute like a ball rico-
cheting off a wall.[2]

The Nash-Fortenberry incident, which quickly
gained considerable attention throughout the nation, has been widely considered to be one of the
genuine and truly unexplained UFO sightings.

## A Call on the Capitol

It happened in the summer of 1952. On Saturday, July 19, just after midnight, eight unknown
objects appeared on the Washington National Airport radar in the restricted air space over the Capi-
tol. A call to the radar technicians at Andrews Air
Force Base confirmed the "pips," whose movements were described by air traffic controller
Harry Barnes as being "completely radical compared to those of ordinary aircraft."

F-94 interceptor jets were immediately scrambled, but as they screamed into the zone, the
UFOs left the scene at speeds calculated to be better than 7,000 miles per hour. Moments after the
jets left the area, the UFOs reappeared on the radar screens. Again the jets were scrambled, and
again the UFOs disappeared.

The hide-and-seek went on for six hours, with
the presence of the UFOs being confirmed by ra-

dar and by visual sightings of strange lights by
both pilots and ground witnesses. Then, as suddenly as they had come, the objects disappeared.

For a week.

The following Saturday, July 26, about 9 p.m.,
the UFOs were back. Again, numerous radar and
visual contacts were made. Again, when the
scrambled F-94s closed in on the lights, they accelerated out of view—with one exception. At one
point, one of the jets was surrounded by the
lights, with the pilot radioing for direction as to
whether he should fire on them. The UFOs did
not take hostile action, but zoomed away from the
plane and several hours later disappeared for good.

The Air Force explanation of the incidents was
that the radar and visual sightings were "due to
mirage effects created by a double temperature inversion."[3]

## UFO Escort

The British Overseas Airways Corporation
(now British Airways) Stratoliner was about three
hours out of New York on its London run, in June
of 1954, when Captain James H. Howard and his
copilot noticed something strange. Off to their left
and approximately three miles away was some un-
invited company: a large elongated object and six
smaller ones. This UFO escort accompanied the
Stratoliner for about eighty miles.

As the plane neared Goose Bay, Labrador for
refueling, Captain Howard radioed the control
tower about what was happening. Upon being in-

formed by ground control, the USAF sent a Sabre fighter to the scene.

"At that," said Captain Howard, "the smaller objects, which had converged on the larger, seemed to enter it, and then the big one shrank." The close-range sighting, which ended in this way, was dismissed by a USAF-sponsored research team as an "optical mirage phenomenon."[4]

## A Brazilian Experience

UFO activity has by no means been confined to North America. Reports of sightings, encounters and abductions have come from around the globe. An abduction of a very bizarre sort is alleged to have occurred in Brazil on October 15, 1957.

Antonio Villas-Boas, a twenty-three-year-old farmer, had along with his two brothers twice sighted bright unidentified objects in the sky in early October. Later, Villas-Boas claimed to have had the following experience:

On the 15th, while plowing at night to avoid the extreme heat of the daytime, he saw a huge egg-shaped luminous object land in front of his tractor. Terrified, he leaped off and ran, only to be grabbed by his arms, lifted from the ground and carried into the object by three figures in tight gray coveralls and helmets. On board the saucer were other occupants who communicated with strange sounds resembling barks or yelps.

Powerless to resist, Villas-Boas was stripped and sponged all over with a liquid. A blood sample was taken from his chin, after which he was left alone in a room with a couch. A short time later an extremely beautiful naked woman entered the room. Villas-Boas became sexually aroused and a passionate encounter took place. He claimed, however, that during the experience the "barking" sounds emitted by the woman gave him "the disagreeable impression that I was with an animal." His clothes were returned to him, he was given a tour of the strange vehicle and was ushered out of the machine. He then watched the UFO vanish. For about a month after the incident, Villas-Boas said he suffered from excessive sleepiness.

This incredible account may well have been regarded as merely the sexual fantasy of a young man were it not for several factors. The medical examination he underwent soon after he reported the encounter revealed, according to Dr. Olavo T. Fontes from the National School of Medicine in Rio de Janeiro, that the young farmer had been exposed to sufficient radiation to produce the kind of poisoning that would normally occur only over a long period of exposure. And at the point where blood was said to have been taken from his chin, the doctor found two small light-colored patches. There the skin looked smoother and thinner, as though it had been renewed.

In addition to this, Villas-Boas was a respected person and appeared to have no desire for publicity. He was, in fact, embarrassed by it, having volunteered information only in general terms when a notice appeared in a newspaper requesting UFO reports. Moreover, Professor Fontes conducted an

extremely thorough investigation which was carefully documented. He concluded that the evidence
for an encounter was genuine. And so the story
has also entered the literature of ufology.[5]

## New Guinea Is Visited

One of the most spectacular sightings in UFO
history occurred in June 1959 on the island of
New Guinea, at a time when the initial excitement
of the late '40s and early '50s was waning under
the pressure of proven hoaxes and intense criticism.

Anglican missionary William Booth Gill, who
had been particularly skeptical of the wave of
UFO sightings which had swept the islands for
about a year, walked out of his mission house
about 6:45 p.m. after dinner on June 26. Glancing
up into the sky he saw "this sparkling object,
which to me was peculiar because it sparkled, and
because it was very bright, and it was above Venus, and so that caused me to watch it for awhile;
then I saw it descend toward us."

Soon Gill was joined by his associate Stephen
Moi and then shortly after by some thirty parish-
ioners. The group watched in amazement as the
light resolved into a huge, four-legged disk-shaped
object which hovered at about 500 feet overhead.
The illuminated forms of four human-like figures
moving about in the craft were seen by the observers. At about 7:30 p.m. the craft ascended into
the clouds, to return an hour later, hovering silently at a lower altitude than previously. This

"mother ship," as Gill later called it, was joined by three smaller UFOs, all of which remained in view until a cloud cover came in about 11 p.m.

At 6 p.m. the next day the mother ship and two of the smaller craft reappeared, again observed by a crowd of witnesses. When Gill and others waved to the occupants they answered with waves. The UFOs remained in view until 7:45 p.m. when clouds again covered the area.

A third visit came the next evening, Sunday, June 28. This time there were eight craft, one of which hovered at a very low altitude. Gill prepared a detailed sighting report which was signed by twenty-five witnesses, all of whom were educated and fluent in English. Many were in leadership positions in the community.

The Royal Australian Air Force declared the sighting to be astronomical and meteorological in nature, an explanation that was rejected by the several dozen credible witnesses and their missionary priest.[6]

## Interrupted Journey

The next truly major UFO event on the North American scene happened in September 1961. The alleged abduction of Barney and Betty Hill in the White Mountains of New Hampshire has been the subject of numerous articles, several movies and the book *The Interrupted Journey* by John G. Fuller.

To recap briefly what has been given voluminous exposure and made the subject of a book, film and TV program is a challenge. Nonetheless, in a nutshell, here is the Hills' story.

On the night of September 19 the Hills were returning from a brief vacation in Canada, driving at night in order to get back to their home in Portsmouth, New Hampshire before the onset of a predicted storm. Just south of Lancaster on Route 4 they observed an unusual light in the sky. Its unpredictable movements caused them to consider, and reject, a variety of explanations for it.

Their curiosity finally led them to stop their car and observe the object with binoculars as it came extremely close to them, appearing to land near the highway in a wooded area. Barney, who had walked toward the object, became frightened. He jumped back into the car and sped off. At that point the Hills heard a strange beeping sound.

They next remembered hearing the same sound some sixty miles down the road, with no memory of the intervening time period of several hours.

Subsequently both Barney and Betty suffered from nightmares and general physical malaise. They strained to remember what had happened during the "blacked-out" period and were troubled by strange shiny spots on the trunk of their car (which caused a compass to react wildly), as well as numerous other inexplicable matters. Barney, in particular, was in denial about the occurrence, but disturbed, along with Betty. Ultimately, in 1964, the Hills underwent hypnosis under the guidance of psychiatrist Benjamin Simon.

Under hypnosis they remembered a long sequence of events involving abduction by a number of small beings who took them aboard the UFO and conducted "medical" examinations on them. Betty recalled being shown a "star map" which she sketched while hypnotized. At first, astronomers couldn't find the star formation, but in 1969, two stars called Zeta 1 and Zeta 2 Reticuli were discovered by astronomers as part of a formation that closely resembled Betty Hill's map. Ufologists see this as definite proof of the reality of the Hill experience and of the existence of extraterrestrials.[7]

## Incident at Exeter

It was 2:24 a.m. on September 3, 1965 when Norman Muscarello, white and shaking, stumbled into the Exeter, New Hampshire police station in a state of near-shock. His story seemed implausible.

While hitchhiking unsuccessfully on Route 150 near Kensington, New Hampshire, the young man—three weeks away from joining the Navy—saw a "thing," as he called it, come noiselessly out of the sky directly toward him. It appeared to be about eighty to ninety feet in diameter with brilliant, pulsating red lights around its rim. Terrified, he ducked down on the shoulder and the object backed off. Making a run for a nearby house, Muscarello got no answer to his pounding and screaming. Shortly after, a middle-aged couple came by in a car and drove him into Exeter, dropping him off at the police station.

Muscarello insisted that a police officer be sent out with him to where he had seen the UFO. Duty Patrolman Reginald Toland, impressed by his obvious sincerity and by a similar report of a sighting through another officer, sent Patrolman Eugene Bertrand out with the extremely nervous young man.

While they were looking around at the site, horses in the stalls at the farm began to kick and whinny and dogs in nearby houses began howling. Again the object appeared, rising from behind some trees, silently wobbling and yawing toward them and bathing the scene in brilliant red light. Ducking into the patrol car, Bertrand startled dispatcher Toland, back at the station, with his call: "My God, I see the d - - - thing myself!"

As Bertrand and Muscarello watched the UFO hover erratically, "dart, turn on a dime, [and] slow down," they were joined by Patrolman David Hunt, who had heard the radio conversations in his cruiser. He, along with the two others, watched the object for several minutes until it moved out of sight toward Hampton. Moments later, the police station received a call from an Exeter operator who had just fielded a call from a hysterical man at a phone booth in Hampton, claiming to have seen a flying saucer.

The incident seemed to trigger a wave of sightings in the area, which were carefully investigated and chronicled in the book *Incident at Exeter* by John G. Fuller. Excerpted in *Reader's Digest*, it became a national bestseller.[8]

## The UFO Chase

One of the most intriguing UFO incidents on record began early on the morning of April 17, 1966. Deputy Sheriff Dale F. Spaur of Portage County, Ohio stopped at a stalled car and spotted above it the bright object that had been reported to his office. He was ordered to follow it. He and an assistant raced after the object in their patrol car for about seventy miles, sometimes being forced to drive at 100 miles per hour in order to keep it in sight.

Forty miles east of the point at which he started, Spaur was joined in the chase by Officer Wayne Huston of East Palestine, with whom he had talked by car radio, and who had also seen the UFO. The chase continued into neighboring Pennsylvania, ending when the object stopped in the town of Conroy. The officers were joined by Conroy policeman Frank Panzanella, who told them that he had been watching the shining object for about ten minutes. All four observers then watched the UFO rise straight up and disappear.

The USAF Project Blue Book, which investigated the case, labeled it as a sighting of Venus, which the officers in question took as an affront to their professional expertise.[9]

## The President Spots a UFO

President Jimmy Carter is one of the most famous persons who claim to have seen a UFO. The incident occurred January 6, 1969, while Carter was governor of Georgia. He and about ten other club members were standing outside the Lions Club in Leary, Georgia where Carter was to give an address at 7:30 p.m. The group observed "a big star, about the same size as the moon, maybe a little smaller. It varied from brighter and larger than a planet to the apparent size of the moon." Initially the round object was stationary and blue in color, but as they watched, it began to rush toward the men, swinging back and forth and turning a deep red. Carter noted that it was luminous but not solid.

Carter did not publicly report the incident until 1973, three years before his election as President. In his campaign for the White House, he promised a full-scale investigation of the UFO phenomenon, a campaign promise he apparently was never able to fulfill. But he did publicly state, "I am convinced that UFOs exist. I have seen one."

Skeptics have calculated that what Carter and his group saw was the planet Venus, which was in the right part of the sky on that date. However, the fact that Carter, who was a trained scientist with a university degree in nuclear physics and had served in the U.S. Navy, did not recognize the common sight of Venus, has called the explanation into question.[10]

Interestingly enough, President Ronald Reagan, when he was governor of California, had a UFO sighting as well. While in the White House Reagan spoke publicly about UFOs on eighteen different occasions.[11]

## The Helicopter and the UFO

It was a calm, clear night on October 18, 1973 when a four-man army reserve helicopter, under the command of Captain Lawrence J. Coyne, left Columbus, Ohio for its home base at the Cleveland Hopkins Airport. It was an experienced crew: Coyne had been flying for nineteen years; First Lieutenant Arrigo Jezzi, flight medic Sergeant John Healy and computer technician Sergeant Robert Yanacsek were veterans.

The copter was cruising at an altitude of 2,500 feet and a speed of ninety knots through a clear, star-filled sky when, about ten miles south of Mansfield, Yanacsek alerted Captain Coyne to a red light on the southeast horizon. Coyne noted the light, which he took to be distant air traffic, and told Yanacsek to keep an eye on it.

Thirty seconds later, Yanacsek reported that the light appeared to be closing in on the copter. To avoid a collision Coyne put their craft into a twenty-degree dive. After initial contact with the Mansfield tower, the radio went dead. As they neared an altitude of 1,700 feet, the object was still on collision course with the copter, and the crew braced for impact. But just as a collision seemed inevitable, the object suddenly stopped about 500 feet above and in front of them.

The soldiers stared in amazement at what was before them: a sixty-foot-long gray metallic object resembling a streamlined fat cigar. At the front was a red light and at the rear a green spotlight which had swung around to envelop the cockpit in green light. "It wasn't cruising, it was stopped—just stopped," reported Yanacsek.

After a few seconds of hovering, the UFO began to accelerate off to the west-northwest, with only a white taillight visible. As the object made a climbing turn and disappeared, Coyne realized to his surprise that his altimeter needle was rising. Though the controls were set for a dive, the copter was rising at 1,000 feet per minute. The helicopter reached nearly 3,800 feet before Coyne regained control. Radio contact was regained at 2,500 feet, and the flight was completed without further incident.

UFO debunker Philip Klass claimed that the Mansfield UFO was really a large fireball of the Orinoid meteor, and that the hovering was illusionary. The helicopter crewmen, who claimed to have watched the object continuously for four or five minutes, were not impressed by Klass' explanation.[12]

## The Pascagoula Incident

The next UFO event to receive a degree of media coverage occurred in Pascagoula, Mississippi on the evening of October 18, 1973. Charles Hickson, forty-nine, and Calvin Parker, nineteen, were fishing from a pier on the banks of the Pascagoula River when they heard a long, drawn-out "zipping" sound. The men turned to see a luminous, gray-blue, egg-shaped craft descend to hover just above the ground about forty feet from the pier.

The astonished men gazed fearfully at the UFO as three bizarre-looking creatures came gliding out of the craft toward them. The two were grabbed by the entities and taken into the ship. Parker was so frightened that he passed out, but Hickson, who retained consciousness, was able to recall receiving an extensive "medical" examination done by the strange creatures. The men were then returned to the pier and the UFO vanished into the night sky with a loud whirring noise.

As Parker regained consciousness, Hickson roared, "I don't believe it! I've got to have a drink to calm my nerves!" After discussion, the pair agreed that they had to tell someone. Finding the newsmen at the Mississippi Daily Press all gone for the night, they telephoned the office of Sheriff Fred Diamond at Jackson County's law-enforcement center. Deputy Captain Glenn Ryder took the call at about 11 p.m. and, impressed by the terror in Parker's voice, asked them to come to the office.

Sheriff Diamond recalled, "As soon as they came through the door, they asked for a lie detector test. The young boy Parker was almost scared to death. He was in a state of near-shock. Both men were frightened and wanted help."

Sheriff Diamond and Captain Ryder listened to Hickson and Parker for several hours, questioning them separately and together. They were also left alone in a room with a hidden tape recorder. "When we put them in the room, they didn't know about the tape recorder," said Ryder. "After I listened to the tapes, I believed them. If they were lying, they should have been in Hollywood because they're the greatest actors I've ever met." During their fear-filled taped conversation Parker was heard fervently praying on several occasions.

The day after the abduction the men went to Kessler Air Force Base for an exam to see if they had radiation contamination, which proved to be negative. Though the pair avoided as much as possible the resulting media crush, they did appear on NBC news to tell their story.

No official investigation into the incident was conducted, though Dr. J. Allen Hynek of The Center for UFO Studies (formerly with the USAF Project Blue Book, but at that point no longer involved in government research) came to Pascagoula to interview the men, as did several other researchers.[13]

## The Walton Case

The forestry crew of six workers loaded their gear onto a truck and set off for home near Heber, Arizona about 6:15 p.m. on November 5, 1975. They had gone only a few yards through the pine forest when one of them pointed out a glow through the trees. At the top of a hill they came to a clearing and the driver stopped in amazement. There, hovering over a woodpile, was an amber, glowing, disc-shaped object. While the rest of the crew stared, twenty-two-year-old Travis Walton jumped out of the truck and moved toward the object.

Suddenly a bright ray of greenish-blue light flashed down from the disc and struck Walton about the head and shoulders, flinging him backward. At this, driver Mike Rogers panicked and drove off at a high speed, but about a quarter of a mile down the road he stopped, and the crew decided that they had to go back to get their friend. They returned, but there was no trace of Walton or the object.

Suspecting foul play when Walton's disappearance was reported, a police investigation and a thorough but unsuccessful search of the area was launched. There seemed to be only three possibilities: Walton was murdered and the fantastic tale was concocted by his companions as a cover-up; a hoax was being perpetrated; or there really had been a paranormal abduction.

Navajo County Sheriff's Deputy Chuck Ellison, who was involved in the questioning of the crew, described them as being "extremely upset," and added: "If they were lying, they were d - - - good actors." One of the crew was so affected he wept. At one point the men passed polygraph tests given by Cy Gilson of the Arizona Department of Public Safety.

Five days later, at 11 p.m. on November 10, Travis Walton called home from a telephone booth a few miles outside Heber. The two family members who picked him up found him distraught and confused, with an unbelievable story to tell. He had a five-day growth of beard and had lost weight.

Walton remembered being struck by the light beam, which jolted him like a bolt of electricity—

then blackness. He awoke in pain, lying on his back staring at a brightly lit ceiling. As he struggled into consciousness, he assumed he had been picked up in the forest and taken to a hospital. When he lifted his head and saw, instead of doctors and nurses, three non-human beings, he panicked and sprang off the table on which he had been lying.

The beings were short, with large hairless heads, huge eyes, small flat noses and slits for mouths.

Walton grabbed a piece of equipment for a weapon, and the beings left the room. He followed them out, down a corridor and into another room which gave him an amazing view of the universe. He sat down in a reclining chair and found that, by operating the controls set in it, he could alter the perspective on billions of stars.

Shortly, a being who looked human and wore a space helmet entered. He ignored Walton's questions and signaled him to follow. They emerged out of the object into a huge "hangar" which housed several other disc-shaped craft. Walton also saw three other "humans"—two men and a woman, all of whom were about six feet tall, with blond hair, golden eyes and tan skin.

Once again Walton asked where he was and what was happening to him, but his questions were ignored. Instead he was directed to lie down, a mask was placed over his face and the blackness returned.

When he came to, he was on the highway outside Heber. A blast of heat hit him from a disk hovering overhead, which then disappeared. He located a telephone and called his brother-in-law.

There has never been an explanation given of the incident. If it is a hoax, the perpetrators have managed to keep quiet about it for over twenty years.[14]

## Teheran Nightmare

The phone calls to the Military Control Center at Teheran, Iran began shortly after midnight on September 19, 1976. The bored duty officer listened impatiently to the excited stories of a bright white light above the city outskirts. He told the callers they were probably watching a bright star; there was nothing to worry about. But the calls persisted, and finally he went out to look for himself. He was startled to see a huge, brilliant, glowing mass hanging above the city.

Calling Shahrokhi Air Base, the officer urged the launch of a Phantom jet interceptor. At 1:30 a.m. the Phantom, piloted by twenty-three-year-old Lieutenant Jafari, took off. Even from seventy miles away, he could see the exceptionally brilliant light. As he closed in on the object Jafari radioed back his account: "It's half the size of the moon . . . radiating colors—violet, orange, white light."

As he drew within a few miles of the monstrous light, it suddenly shot away. He attempted to catch it but was easily outdistanced. Frustrated, he radioed Shahrokhi Base and was directed to abandon pursuit and return home.

Moments later Jafari radioed: "Something is coming at me. . . . I think it's going to crash into me." Then, after moments of tension, an obviously shaken pilot announced, "It's just passed by—missing me narrowly." The terrified pilot was stunned by the experience and, disoriented and confused, had to be shepherded back to the base by the tower personnel.

Meanwhile a second Phantom had been scrambled and headed toward the UFO location. As before, when the jet approached the object it shot away at incredible speed. This time, however, the UFO ejected a ball of light that headed for the Phantom. The pilot attempted to launch an AIM 9 heat-seeking missile at the object, but experienced power failure. The UFO "missile" bore down on the now defenseless jet, but at the last moment did an impossible U-turn and headed back to the source.

The UFO next ejected a second ball of light onto the desert floor, where it illuminated a large area as though it were day. The object then instantaneously accelerated to an utterly fantastic speed and disappeared at an estimated rate of thousands of miles an hour. There was no repeat visit.

The incident was taken seriously, being considered credible, but no explanation has ever been made public.[15]

## A Frenchman "Loses" a Week

In the early hours of November 26, 1979, Franck Fontaine disappeared from Cergy-Pontoise, France, while helping two friends load a station wagon with clothes to be sold at an outdoor market. Shortly before Fontaine came up missing, his friends Pierre Prevost and Salomon N'Diaye witnessed a great ball of light surround the car and finally shoot up into the sky. Subsequently they found that Fontaine was gone.

Badly shaken, the two went to report to the police, a remarkable action in itself, since they were driving a car with no license and were generally considered to be "on the fringe of the law." Fontaine could not be located, despite a widespread search. Speculation was rife, and the disappearance garnered worldwide media coverage.

A week later Fontaine awoke to find himself in a cabbage field near where he had been abducted. Only after he had walked to his apartment and met his friends did he realize he had been gone for a week. Later he had vague recollections of having been aboard some strange craft. The local chief of police declared he had no reason to disbelieve the young men's story.

Invited to be hypnotized, Fontaine declined. His friend Prevost volunteered to "stand in" for him, and under hypnosis declared that he, Prevost, had been selected to be a spokesman for the aliens who had abducted Fontaine! Subsequently he formed a short-lived organization, and then several years later announced that it had all been a fraud.

Fontaine and N'Diaye were incensed at the "confession," maintaining that the experience was real. Jimmy Guiew, bestselling author of over twenty titles in France, who had written a book on the incident, also maintained—on the basis of his investigation—that it was an actual event.

The mystery remains.[16]

## Crop Circles

The overnight appearance of circles and patterns of flattened grain in farm fields around the world has been recorded since medieval times. An example of this is the seventeenth-century woodcut called "The Mowing Devil," which depicts an obviously diabolical figure creating circles in a grain field. The crop circles have been a strange mystery. Because of the increased prevalence of the phenomenon in the 1980s, a tremendous amount of speculation that they are related to UFO activity has been generated.

The Circles Effect Research Group (CERES), headed by founder J. Meaden, a world authority on crop circles, gathers reports from all over the globe. The patterns vary. In the U.S. they tend to be small simple circles, while in Europe the circles are generally larger, often with added abstract designs. Sizes vary from a foot and a half to 200 feet in diameter. And while the circles are found all over the world, particularly in Australia, France, Japan and the U.S., they are most frequently found in the British counties of Wiltshire and Hampshire.

It has been suggested that these mysterious physical effects are actually landing sites for UFOs. That view was strenghtened by the fact

that many crop circle manifestations were reportedly preceded by eyewitness accounts of eerie
lights, strange noises and UFO sightings. Whatever they are and however they are created, their
existence is a well-documented fact, with not all of
the various explanations for their appearance
proving to be completely satisfactory.[17]

Skeptics certainly feel convinced, as will be
noted later, that there are logical explanations:
either natural causes or—more particularly—
elaborate hoaxes.

However, other independent researchers, such
as Nelson Pacheco and Tommy Blann, authors of
*Unmasking the Enemy*, point out that documented
crop circle reports date back to the 1960s, long before any claimed activity by hoaxers, and that
many carefully investigated cases—often in conjunction with cattle mutilations—cannot be explained.[18]

## Those Mysterious Mutilations

Another mysterious and controversial phenomenon, which in the minds of many observers
is linked to UFOs, is the widespread rash of cattle
mutilations in recent years.

The mutilations have certain characteristics in
common: no footprints are ever found around
the carcasses; various body parts, including organs, are invariably missing, cut from the body
very precisely and surgically; the body is devoid
of blood, yet no blood is found on or about the
animal; and the phenomenon is widespread—

without, at this point, any satisfactory conclusive solution.

Ufologists believe that extraterrestrials are responsible, needing blood and organs for a variety of suggested reasons.

Pacheco and Blann have done a great deal of excellent and detailed research on the subject. Their reasoned conclusion is that the mutilations are the work of satanic cults, frequently using helicopters to obtain blood and body parts for use in evil rituals. They believe that the scope of such evil activity extends beyond animal mutilation to include humans—documenting a number of murder/mutilations that are identical in their characteristics to the widespread animal mutilations.[19]

Pacheco and Blann reproduce the gist of *Jay's Journal*, a book edited by child psychologist Beatrice Sparks, as further evidence in support of their position.

*Jay's Journal* is the diary of a sixteen-year-old boy who committed suicide. It describes his involvement in drugs and occult practices, including cattle mutilations, which ultimately led him to such despair that he shot himself. The despair, according to Sparks, came as Jay discovered that he was no longer in control of whatever he'd become involved in—it was controlling him!

Jay revealed in his diary the attraction that the occult had—the mystical, luring effect that took him deeper and deeper into the preternatural until he had no control over it. He and his high school friends were eventually led to a group that was mutilating cattle in order to obtain the sex organs and blood for ritualistic ceremonies. He described the mutilations and ceremonies they held later with the body parts and blood. He also wrote of a mysterious orange light and other mind-bending paranormal events he had witnessed during certain ritualistic ceremonies.

Jay had many paranormal experiences while delving into the occult, until one night he came face-to-face with the demons behind it all. His journal describes how he was lying in bed when he felt the presence of something staring at him. He got up and tried to turn on all the lights in the room but they wouldn't work except for one small night-light which remained on. He got on his knees to pray, but felt that the presence didn't want him to pray. Breathing heavily, Jay looked up in fear; he saw a slim, short, gray-skinned being which appeared to be wearing a "kind of tight-fitting gray jumpsuit thing." (The similarity between UFO abductees' descriptions of aliens and Jay's description of this being and its characteristics is amazing.)

The being spoke to Jay telepathically, telling him that he was "Raul" and that he wanted Jay's body. After saying it would be back, the being disappeared.

Jay was terrified. He knew that he had gotten in too deep and felt that there was no way out. After completing final entries in his journal "so that maybe someone would know the horrible truth," Jay committed suicide.[20]

## UFO Best-sellers

*Communion*, the account of writer Whitley Strieber's UFO abduction, was published in January 1987. It quickly became one of the most successful books in publishing history and certainly the best-selling UFO book ever, rapidly rising to the number one position on the *New York Times* best-seller list and remaining there for months. The book's compelling cover picture of an alien with huge almond-shaped black eyes seemed to be everywhere.

It spawned a major motion picture (which bombed at the box office but is still being seen via cable and video rentals) as well as the sequels *Transformation* and *Breakthrough*. Strieber's books and the subsequent publicity tours generated tremendous interest in the UFO abduction experience. Hitchhiking on the popularity of *Communion*, Strieber set up a support network for abductees and published a newsletter entitled *Communion Letter*. By 1995 he had received 139,000 written responses!

Understandably, Strieber became the darling of the ufologists. However, tensions developed between him and the UFO community, and in 1990 he discontinued his newsletter and withdrew from public view for a period of about five years. During this time he wrote *Breakthrough*, published in late 1995, in which he claims he has been given significant further guidance from the extraterrestrials concerning Earth's future.

Strieber had his initial abduction experience in his upstate New York cabin on December 26, 1985. It, and succeeding experiences, troubled him to the point of his contemplating suicide until he underwent hypnosis with abductee researcher and author Budd Hopkins. Convinced of the reality of what had happened to him, Strieber devoted himself to understanding and responding to the entities who were visiting him. In the process, his writings have dramatically advanced the UFO abduction profile in the public mind.[21]

These stories do not begin to exhaust the volume of UFO literature. And as we see in the next chapter, the reports appear to be increasing.

# CHAPTER THREE

# *The Tip of the Iceberg*

The UFO incidents and experiences described in chapter 2 are only a tiny fraction of the millions reported, and only a fraction of the hundreds of dramatic accounts. The editor of *UFO Magazine*, in responding to a reader's letter in the November/December 1996 issue, wrote: "If I were to spend 24 hours a day for the next 30 years plowing through books and archives on UFOs, I couldn't possibly hope to read and digest the voluminous information that currently exists." While he is undoubtedly exaggerating, it is nevertheless a fact that there is an incredible amount of UFO material in existence. Scores of books and magazines, like *Fate, The Flying Saucer Digest, UFO Magazine, The Unopened Files* and more, are full of UFO stories.

Stories like these:

*The Lubbock Lights.* A spate of sightings of eighteen to twenty unexplained white lights in V formation occurred in Lubbock, Texas near midnight on August 30, 1951. In addition to scores of witnesses, the lights were documented by a 35mm photo taken by Carl Hart, Jr. The photo, which has been subjected to extensive investigation, is considered to be genuine.[1]

*Officer Zamora Sighting.* On April 24, 1964, Socorro, New Mexico policeman Lonnie Zamora, investigating a bluish flame and roaring sound near a dynamite shack in a gully, witnessed a landed UFO with two small "people" by it. As he described it to his dispatcher by car radio, the vehicle took off. Other police arrived within moments; the physical evidence supported Zamora's claim that something had indeed been in the gully.[2]

*Minnesota Incident.* August 27, 1979, 1:40 a.m.: Marshall County Deputy Sheriff Val Johnson, heading down a county highway to investigate a light in an isolated area, was "rushed" by the light and lapsed into unconsciousness to the sound of breaking glass. At 2:19 a.m. he radioed the dispatcher's office, having just regained consciousness. Asked what happened, he said, "I don't know. Something just hit my car." Officers arriving on the scene found extensive damage: a seriously cracked windshield, bent antenna, smashed lights and more. Both the vehicle's clock and Johnson's wristwatch were running fourteen minutes slow. Johnson's eyes hurt badly, as if from welding burns, according to an examining doctor. No explanation has been forthcoming.[3]

*The Vanishing F-89.* In November 1953, U.S. Air

Force pilot Lieutenant Felix Moncla, Jr. and radar man Lieutenant R.R. Wilson were sent aloft from Kinross Air Force Base near Michigan's Soo Locks in their F-89 all-weather interceptor. Their mission: track a UFO spotted on radar, flying at 500 miles per hour over Lake Superior. The airmen were never heard from again. The last trace of them was on radar, which showed them approaching an altitude of 8,000 feet as they passed over Keweenaw Point. At that moment, their "blip" and that of the UFO converged, then disappeared. One of the radar officers said, "It seems incredible, but the blip apparently swallowed our F-89." No satisfactory explanation has ever been made, and the case remains an "unknown" to this day.[4]

*The Proposed UFO Landing Field.* The little town of Elmwood, Wisconsin, near Eau Claire, gained national notoriety in 1988 when a plan to build a "UFO Landing Field and Welcome Center" near the town was announced. The scheme, dreamed up by a local entrepreneur, grew out of several dramatic UFO sightings in the vicinity.

The most remarkable of these involved policeman George Wheeler. While on patrol, the officer called in on his radio that he had sighted an enormous UFO, a call that was interrupted because the radio went dead. When he was reached, the dazed Wheeler reported that a blue ray from the UFO had hit his car as the object took off and disappeared. The car's lights, radio, points and spark plugs were ruined. The badly shaken Wheeler was examined by his doctor and released, but continued to suffer from headaches. He was hospitalized for eleven days in Eau Claire, undergoing inconclusive tests; after six pain-filled months, during which he repeatedly insisted he had radiation poisoning, George Wheeler died.[5]

*The Falcon Lake Burn.* Steve Michalak, a fifty-two-year-old mechanic whose hobby was geology, was prospecting near Falcon Lake, eighty miles east of Winnipeg, Manitoba on May 20, 1967. Just after lunch he observed two UFOs descend, one of which landed, while the other returned to the sky and rapidly disappeared from sight. Steve watched the stationary UFO through the welding goggles he used to protect his eyes from rock chips, making several sketches of it. Concluding the craft was a secret experimental airship, he approached it. As he did, a blast of heat from a vent struck him, knocking him down and setting his shirt on fire. The UFO took off and disappeared. He rolled on the ground to extinguish the flames.

Feeling dazed and nauseous, he gathered up his things and walked two miles to the Trans-Canada Highway, vomiting frequently as he went. Back in Winnipeg he was hospitalized and treated for first-degree burns—the beginning of a mysterious eighteen-month illness. He lost weight, developed a rash, suffered nausea and blackouts, and three months later had the pattern of a grille appear on his chest. Tests for radiation contamination proved negative, but no official explanation of the experience has ever been provided.[6]

*Woodbridge and Bentwaters, Suffolk, England incident.* Early in the morning of December 27, 1980, two USAF security police stationed at the Woodbridge Royal Air Force Base saw unusual lights in the Rendlesham Forest at the rear of the base. Fearing that an aircraft may have gone down, they requested permission to investigate. Three patrolmen were allowed to do so.

The men reported coming upon a strange glowing object among the trees: a triangular, metallic-like craft which illuminated the entire forest around it with a white light. It appeared to be hovering near the ground, with a pulsing red light on top and a bank of blue lights underneath it. At the approach of the men the object maneuvered rapidly through the woods and disappeared, during which time animals on a nearby farm went into a frenzy. The UFO was sighted briefly about an hour later near the back gate of the base.

Three depressions in the ground were discovered where the craft had been sighted. When checked for radiation the readings were positive, with a peak reading in the center of the triangle of depressions.

Later on the night of December 28 a red sun-like light, pulsing and moving about, was seen through the trees of the forest. It separated into five white objects and disappeared. Immediately thereafter three star-like objects were sighted in the sky. Moving in sharp angular fashion, they displayed red, green and blue lights, with one periodically beaming down a stream of light.

A number of Air Force personnel witnessed these activities, which lasted for more than an hour. The entire experience was reported in a detailed memo dated January 13, 1981, by Colonel Charles Halt, USAF, Deputy Base Commander, who lists himself as one of the witnesses.[7]

## The Stories Keep Coming

The list seems endless.

*Swiss sighting*. There's Eduard "Billy" Meier, the Swiss farmer, who in 1976 began to release convincing photos of UFOs hovering over the Swiss countryside. Along with the photos the one-armed, illiterate Meier told about contacts with a beautiful woman named Semjase, an extraterrestrial from the planet Erra in the Pleiades, of the Seven Sisters cluster. Though later denounced as a fraud by his own wife, Meier attracted a huge worldwide following, many of whom not only accepted his story, but visited him in Switzerland—some remaining to become part of his compound.[8]

*UFO photo*. On May 11, 1950, Paul Trent of McMinnville, Oregon took two photographs of a large metallic disk, which both Mr. and Mrs. Trent witnessed flying over their farm. Regarding this case, a government-appointed commission reported:

> This is one of the few UFO reports in which all factors investigated, geometric, psychological and physical, appear to be consistent with the assertion that an extraor-

dinary flying object, silvery, metallic, disk-shaped, tens of meters in diameter and evidently artificial, flew within sight of two witnesses.[9]

*NORAD.* Inside Cheyenne Mountain near Colorado Springs, Colorado is a huge man-made cave, over 2,500 feet deep, which houses the U.S. Space Command's Space Surveillance Center. This sophisticated technological marvel constantly monitors the traffic whizzing through space—for all of which there is precise accounting. The total number of orbiting objects is known and identified.

Of particular concern is the area inside the "fence" around the U.S. Stretching 3,000 miles across the southern United States from Georgia to California and extending 1,000 miles off each coast, this fence is actually a man-made energy field that reaches out nearly 15,000 miles into space. Transmitters located around the nation send out continuous fan-shaped waves of radio energy. This surveillance network is known as NORAD—the *NOR*th *A*merican *D*efense system.

When an unidentified, or "bogey," object passes through this beam, the energy field is tripped. The various transmitters lock in on the object to determine its size and speed. This information, processed by computer, is relayed to the Cheyenne Center for analysis and action.

The energy field has frequently been tripped by unidentified objects—objects which go through many different series of complex maneuvers and rapid changes of inclination at speeds and altitudes that are "impossible." There appears to be no valid explanation.[10]

*Astronaut sightings.* The comments of several of the U.S. astronauts concerning their UFO sightings have frequently been made public. Buzz Aldrin, Gordon Cooper, Alan Bean, Pete Conrad, Dick Gordon, Edgar Mitchell and John Young (currently special assistant to the director of the Johnson Space Center), have all gone on record as having seen UFOs around their craft in space.[11] In fact, fifteen astronauts in all have sighted UFOs. A number of the objects were observed moving, or orbiting, east to west—something no man-made satellite could do. *Apollo 11* recorded "weird howling sounds in space" for which there was no explanation.

James Lovell and Frank Borman in *Gemini 7*, December 1965, reported a UFO sighting during their fourteenth orbit. When Gemini control suggested it was the final stage of their own Titan booster, they indicated that they had *both* the booster and the UFO in sight.[12]

On March 24, 1989, John Blaha, commander of the *Discovery* space shuttle, transmitted the following report (intercepted by an amateur): "Houston, this is *Discovery*. We still have the alien spacecraft under observation."[13]

Astronaut Mitchell's statement is intriguing: "We all know that UFOs are real. All we need to ask is where do they come from."[14]

It should be noted, however, that skeptics point

to the fact that careful and thorough research has fairly well established that most astronaut UFO reports can be explained as other satellites or debris in orbit. Certainly none of the sightings were of a classic "disk with a dome," or manifested any of the defining UFO characteristics, such as incredible acceleration or right-angle turns.[15]

Nevertheless, Mitchell, on NBC's "Dateline," said he had met several official people who have had personal UFO encounters with ETs. Mitchell commented, "I think the evidence is very strong and large portions of it are classified."[16]

## There's a Religious Element

In the midst of all the furor over UFO sightings and contacts, and from the earliest days of the modern era, there has been—not surprisingly—a strong religious element, perhaps better termed a cultic aspect.

To completely document the variety of such UFO-related groups would be virtually impossible, given their number. Such documentation alone would certainly require a book-length treatment and is far beyond the scope of this volume. However, a brief summary of some of the better-known and/or more bizarre will give an idea of how extensive has been the UFO cult element.

*The Venusian visitor.* The date was November 20, 1952. George Adamski—a luminary of sorts on the southern California scene, having founded, in the mid-1930s, a quasi-religious group called The Royal Order of Tibet, as well as lecturing on "uni-

versal law" on radio and before live audiences—
contacted an exterrestrial! It happened in the desert where Adamski and six of his followers had
gone with the express desire of seeing UFOs and
hopefully meeting their occupants.

Adamski was alone when he encountered a
handsome Venusian, who gave him a tour of his
parked spacecraft and—via sign language and telepathy—said that the UFOnauts (a term used for
occupants of UFOs) were coming to warn earthlings to cease their warlike ways, particularly nuclear testing.

Though Adamski had no witnesses or photos
(one of his cameras was out of focus and the other
malfunctioned, leaving him only one very blurry
shot), his account of the contact by the "space
brothers"—ongoing via telepathy—launched him
into a round of radio, TV and personal appearances and the authorship of two best-sellers.

Adamski gained a fairly large following for his
"Cosmic Philosophy" cult, whose members were
"brainwashed to believe that the 'space brothers'
were here in their UFOs, preparing to make open
contact with Earth and usher in a 'New Age' of
peace and harmony."[17] Members were told that if
they left the group, whose beliefs came primarily
from a blend of Tibetan and theosophical philosophy, they would die.

The UFO Education Center, located in Wisconsin until 1980, when it was exposed by the media for its requirement that members devote
"every waking moment" to educating the world

about the "space brothers," was a continuing Adamski legacy.[18]

*A "messiah" from California.* A man called "The Berkley Messiah," Allen-Michael Noonan, surfaced about the same time as Adamski, and founded what he called "The One World Family." He claimed to be a messiah and "the very spirit of the Archangel Michael." His "cosmic initiation" began in 1947—the year the UFO sightings gained prominence—and continued through telepathic communication with the extraterrestrials piloting the UFOs. An ambitious attempt to produce a massive twelve-volume document entitled *To the Youth of the World* was edited by a fellow UFO contactee after being dictated through automatic writing. What the Venusian spirits dictated was a mishmash of occult philosophy mixed with the biblical book of Revelation.[19]

*The voice of the "interplanetary parliament."* Dr. George King, who combined elements of yoga, Christianity and ufology to found the Aetherius Society in 1956, had a previous reputation as an occult spiritual healer. He became proficient at going into trance states, during which he received messages from Aetherius—the "space master from the planet Venus." His society, which still has branches in Europe and Australia as well as the United States, undertakes "benevolent acts" through metaphysical rituals such as "Operation Prayer Power" in which "energy derived through contact with extraterrestrials is channeled into prayer boxes which are then beamed to the

world's trouble spots." The work of the Society is
to prepare the way for the coming of the next
Master—an alien who will be "mightier than all
earth's armies and who will 'remove from the
earth' all who refuse to heed his words."[20]

*PR agent for the Maitreya.* In 1960 Benjamin
Creme became a UFO contactee when he saw a
"beam of light and met Space Brothers" who told
him that he was chosen for a special mission.[21]
Partial fulfillment of that mission led to the announcements, in the early 1980s and onward, that
the Lord Maitreya, the World Teacher known by
Christians as Christ, the Jews as the Messiah,
Buddhists as the Fifth Buddha, Muslims as the
Iman Mahdi and Hindus as Krishna—all, he says,
names for one individual—has been in the world,
literally, since 1977. As the representative and a
leader of the Tara Center, Creme was responsible
for the placement of such announcements in a
number of the leading newspapers of the world,
such as *The New York Times, USA Today* and others. He has appeared widely to tell the world that
Lord Maitreya is "now here," and will be fully revealed when the time is ripe.[22]

*AWOL cultists.* The six soldiers from the 701st
Military Intelligence Brigade who went AWOL in
July 1990 from a National Security Agency post
in Germany and somehow showed up in Gulf
Breeze, Florida, location of long-standing reports
of UFO sightings, belonged to another cult—the
little-known "The End of the World" group. One
of the six, Vance Davis, admitted that their deser-

tion was directed by "ouija board spirits [who] told them they needed their help to lead the world through an impending crisis." The locating of the Antichrist and the UFO-related "rapture of the church" were part of the spirit revelations. The high-level security clearances all six held drew the attention of the CIA, the National Security Agency and the FBI before a lid was clamped on media reporting of the strange sequence of events.[23]

Of course, the "Heaven's Gate" cult—undoubtedly the most widely known of the UFO cults—also got its start years ago. Though having a more dramatically tragic ending, "Heaven's Gate" was not all that different from the vast majority of past and present groups.

## Only the Fringe

And still we've touched only the fringe. Sightings have been, and are, reported in Russia, France, Israel, England, Mexico, Canada, Belgium, South America—the list seems endless. The remarkable series of UFO encounters at Copley Woods, near Indianapolis;[24] the Gulf Breeze, Florida encounters;[25] the enormous number of animal mutilations, unexplained phenomena and UFO sightings in the rugged western San Luis Valley, site of a great deal of Native American lore[26]—all are only a tiny part of the vast body of UFO literature.

"UFO Chronicles of the Soviet Union: A Cosmic Samizdat," published in 1992, documents Jacques Vallee's investigation of the UFO situation in the Soviet Union. In particular the widely reported sightings at Voronezh, Russia in September 1989, are described. The incident, in which a number of children reported witnessing the landing of a huge red sphere from which a ten-foot-tall being and a robot emerged, has been strongly attacked by skeptics as spurious, though Vallee vouches for its authenticity.[27]

The variety of UFO encounters seems almost as great as the number reported.

*UFOS and the Limits of Science* by Ronald D. Story is a hard, skeptical look at a number of the more famous UFO sightings up to the end of the 1970s.[28] Story, in company with the debunkers, brands many of these as hoaxes or explainable in terms of natural or scientific causes.

However, in the second half of his book Story undertakes an examination of the "ten most baffling UFO cases on record." In addition to eight which we've included in our review of UFO events, Story cites the 1979 New Year's Day New Zealand TV crew's filming, from a plane, of fifty minutes of UFO activity. He also includes the widely witnessed landing of a UFO at Levelland, Texas on November 2 and 3, 1957.

Story concludes that these ten, as well as others which he did not examine in detail, pose questions whose answers lie "beyond the limits of modern science" to explain. In other words—these UFO events are truly unidentified and inexplicable.

## UFO Sightings Classified

Classification of this enormous variety of experiences was first enunciated by Dr. J. Allen Hynek, the astronomer who was a consultant to Project Blue Book and later co-founder of The Center for UFO Studies. Hynek developed three categories of encounters:

- Close Encounters of the First Kind (CE1), which describes any sighting of a UFO, with or without occupants, at close range, 500 feet or less.
- Close Encounters of the Second Kind (CE2) involve UFOs which leave physical evidence on the environment, such as landing marks, broken tree limbs or bushes, scorched earth and so on.
- Close Encounters of the Third Kind (CE3) are sightings of UFOs with occupants, at very close range, including landed craft with apparently intelligent beings in or about the vehicle. Interaction between human contactees and UFO occupants fall into this category.[29]

Over the years Hynek's basic classification (which was the basis for the title of the movie *Close Encounters of the Third Kind*) has been added to, and somewhat modified by investigators. Included now are:

- Close Encounters of the Fourth Kind (CE4),

which involve alleged abductions by UFOs in which people are involuntarily taken aboard a UFO. Usually various physical "examinations" and "experiments" are conducted. Claims are often made for the physical evidence of such tests in the form of unusual scars, bruises or unexplained pain, as well as vague memories of the experiences. Often, however, such episodes are "forgotten" until something such as a hypnotic session uncovers the memory of the abduction.[30]

Still other students of UFO phenomena have included several more categories. John Ankerberg and John Weldon in their book *The Facts on UFOs and Other Supernatural Phenomena* add two:

- Close Encounters of the Fifth Kind (CE5), which involve "abductees" who claim to be in personal contact with UFO entities, typically through occult means.
- Close Encounters of the Sixth Kind (CE6), which include those who have suffered serious injuries or death from a UFO close encounter.[31]

It's obviously a vast field. In fact, UFO phenomena are so complex that Jacques Vallee in *Confrontations: A Scientist's Search for Alien Contact* has advocated a twenty-point classification system in order to better analyze the information.[32]

## The Number Is Increasing

And the encounters keep happening—apparently with increasing frequency.

In 1975 Hynek estimated that there were some 100 sightings a night somewhere around the world.[33] By way of comparison, the November/December 1996 issue of *UFO Magazine* carried an extensive report titled "The 1996 British UFO Wave." Prefacing the lengthy series of reported sightings, the article noted that 1996 had seen a "huge increase" in the number of UFO sightings, not only in Britain, but also in Brazil, Mexico, Israel, South Africa and Australia. The editors noted that all indications were that the year would be a record one for encounters.[34]

The magnitude of the subject, and the interest it creates, may be further seen in the number and variety of UFO-related publications and events. Phil Cousineau, in his book *UFOs: A Manual for the Millennium*, lists eight bona fide UFO organizations in the U.S. and thirteen internationally; ten annual UFO conferences; fifteen monthly or bimonthly magazines; eight major resource centers or services; and twenty-eight web sites.[35] Though published only two years ago, Cousineau's figures are seriously dated; a typical web search, for example, reveals scores of internet listings on UFOs.

Obviously, *something* is happening.

But what?

Are these experiences *real*, or are they the product of widespread fantasies for which there are logical, rational explanations?

Chapter 4 looks at the answers offered.

# CHAPTER FOUR

# *The Debate Rages*

The subject of UFOs unquestionably polarizes most people who have any knowledge of the phenomenon. It's been so virtually from day one, when the Arnold "flying saucer" sighting hit the media.

Apart from those who have no interest in the subject, the public is clearly divided into believers and skeptics, although within each camp there is a wide range of viewpoints.

Some, who began research as skeptics, have become believers. Notable among such is the late J. Allen Hynek, who was introduced in the previous chapter. Professor emeritus and a former chairman of the astronomy department at Northwestern University, Hynek had a reputation as a skeptical observer of the early '50s rash of saucer sightings. That reputation was to change, as we will note later.

The polarization over UFOs surfaced quickly at the very outset of the modern era of sightings.

Kenneth Arnold, whose description of nine UFOs seen near Mount Ranier launched the first wide-spread UFO publicity, was regarded by many as a "kook," while others wholeheartedly accepted his story.

Within two weeks that polarization would be even more apparent in the excitement over the Roswell "UFO crash." A day after an Air Force public relations officer announced that a crashed UFO had been captured, the military corrected that statement and offered an official explanation for the crash debris. This action, which sparked vigorous disagreement from area residents and from ufologists, apparently set the course for the ongoing government position of denial of the existence of UFOs.

## Investigation Is Launched

However, the public interest in the wave of flying saucer sightings, coupled with growing demands for answers, prompted the U.S. government to take action. To allay fears and quell rumors of a threat to national security, the military undertook several official investigations. The first of these, in 1947, was called Project Sign. It was replaced by Project Grudge in 1949, which in turn gave way to Project Twinkle in 1950. The best-known, and by far the longest-lasting, of these Air Force investigations was launched in 1951. Dubbed Project Blue Book, it continued until 1969.

Project Blue Book gathered over 25,000 reports

of UFO sightings. The vast majority of these were judged to be of objects which had a logical explanation. Critics, however, claimed that most of the reports were investigated only superficially or not at all. But it was a statement by Dr. Hynek, which he later claimed was misinterpreted by the media, that created the greatest furor over Blue Book.

Hynek seemed to be an excellent choice by the Air Force for inclusion in Project Blue Book. A graduate of the University of Chicago, he had moved steadily up the ladder of his scholarly discipline, through professorship at Ohio State University to associate directorship of the Smithsonian Astrophysical Observatory at Harvard, finally becoming the astronomy department chairman and director of the observatory at Northwestern University. In addition, he provided distinguished service to the U.S. space program, organizing a worldwide network called Operation Moonwatch, to enable NASA to track satellites.

Moreover, Hynek apparently shared the skepticism of both the Air Force and the scientific community concerning the rash of saucer sightings. However, when a flurry of UFO sightings took place at Ann Arbor, Michigan in 1966, both Hynek and Project Blue Book garnered a great deal of ridicule and negative publicity. It happened when Hynek, just arrived on the scene, fatigued and poorly briefed at the time, suggested that the sightings were attributable to "swamp gas." His words became a catch phrase, used in mockery.

The upshot of the gaffe was that then-Representative Gerald Ford felt forced to call for an independent scientific investigation of the UFO situation. Six leading scientists, including Hynek and Carl Sagan, were appointed to the commission. Headed by Edward Condon, who indicated clearly from the outset that he was biased against the existence of UFOs, the final Condon Report was received in a fashion which definitely reinforced the polarization.

After investigating only eighty-seven of the 25,000 cases collected by Project Blue Book, Condon's summary was published in 1969. The report asserted that "all careful consideration of the record . . . leads us to conclude that further extensive study of UFOs probably cannot be justified on the expectation that science will be advanced thereby."[1] Project Blue Book was discontinued shortly thereafter.

## Hynek Reacts

Hynek's response to the report was one of outrage. In the *Bulletin of Atomic Scientists*, he wrote that

> . . . both the public and the project staff apparently have confused the UFO problem with the ETH (extraterrestrial intelligence hypothesis). This may hold the greatest popular interest, but it is not the issue. The issue is: Does a legitimate UFO phenomenon exist? It may be that the UFO phenom-

ena are . . . inexplicable in twentieth-century physics. From this point of view how does the Condon Report serve science when it suggests that a phenomenon which has been reported by many thousands of people over so long a time is unworthy of ongoing scientific attention?[2]

A further insight into Hynek's frame of mind is obtained from a statement he made in an article in a 1984 issue of *OMNI* magazine. He wrote:

When you get reports from professors at MIT, engineers on balloon projects, military and commercial pilots, and air-traffic controllers, you might one day sit down and say to yourself, "Just how long am I going to keep calling all these people crazy?"[3]

Hynek had been surprised to find in his work with Project Blue Book that the majority of UFO reports were from pilots, ship's officers, police officers and technicians—people trained to be observant and analytical. Increasingly as the months went by he became chagrined and disappointed that the scientific world wasn't sufficiently "agog, furiously curious and anxious for answers." In 1972 he wrote *The UFO Experience: A Scientific Inquiry* and by 1973 he had become a "reformed ufologist."

That year, motivated by another wave of sightings and by the "caliber of witnesses" whom he had met in the past twenty-two years, Hynek and Sherman J. Larsen co-founded the Center for UFO Studies (CUFOS). He directed the Center until his death of cancer in 1986.

In the 1950s the most forceful critic of the USAF's continuing claim that UFOs were not real was retired Marine Corps Major Donald E. Keyhoe. His "prodding and poking" frequently caused Pentagon UFO debunkers great consternation.

A respected aviation journalist, Keyhoe wrote an explosive article entitled "The Flying Saucers Are Real!" for the January 1950 issue of the widely read men's magazine *True*. Not only were UFOs real, Keyhoe maintained, but the Air Force knew it and was conspiring to cover up the truth. Keyhoe claimed to have gathered leaked information from his Washington contacts concerning encounters between military interceptor aircraft and fast-moving disks—as well as evidence of official concern about such events.

In 1959, after writing three best-selling books on UFOs and the "cover-up," Keyhoe became director of the National Investigative Committee on Aerial Phenomena (NICAP), continuing his crusade to obtain official recognition of the reality of the UFO phenomena. Keyhoe served as NICAP director until his retirement in 1969.[4]

A more recent skeptic-turned-believer is Nick Pope, the man who from 1991 to 1994 was responsible for investigating and analyzing claims of UFO sightings for the British Ministry of Defense. During this period, Pope worked for the

Secretariat (Air Staff) Department 2A—"The UFO Desk." In 1996 he wrote *Open Skies, Closed Minds: For the First Time a Government UFO Expert Speaks Out*. In it he declares that, originally very skeptical, he was forced by the sheer weight of evidence to acknowledge that extraterrestrial spacecraft really are routinely breaching the United Kingdom's air defenses and that they represent a major potential threat to national security. He details what he believes to be the evidence for his position.[5]

## Research Abounds

Before CUFOS was founded, a number of other research groups were already in existence. Among those which took a sympathetic view of the UFO phenomena were NICAP, the Aerial Phenomena Research Organization (APRO) and the Mutual UFO Network, Inc. (MUFON). Of the three, only MUFON is still in existence today and claims to be the world's largest UFO membership organization.

An international scientific network of people seriously interested in studying and researching the UFO phenomenon, MUFON sponsors and conducts worldwide conferences, seminars and symposiums, including the annual International UFO Symposium. They produce a variety of publications. MUFON also engages in the training of UFO investigators and others interested in research. MUFONET is their computer bulletin board system on the internet.[6]

While philosophically committed to objectivity, MUFON undoubtedly fits best into the camp of the believers as the oldest of the current research groups.

## The Skeptics

There are skeptics, however. And some feel compelled to battle what they perceive to be the irrationality and superstition of the believers. They've been dubbed "the debunkers."

Phil Klass, universally acknowledged to be the chief of these for three decades, became involved in the fray almost incidentally in the summer of 1966.

Klass, an editor with the Washington-based *Aviation and Space Technology Week*, was comfortably ensconced in a challenging and rewarding career, with no interest in UFOs, when he happened to scan John Fuller's *Incident at Exeter.*

He was convinced that Fuller and his subjects were wrong. They had seen ball lightning, not alien spaceships; and the radar blips were generated by the overhead cables near each of the sightings!

Klass wrote a book review designed to set the record straight, as he saw it. It appeared in the August 22, 1966 issue of *Aviation Week* and made him an "instant authority" on the UFO phenomena. Shortly thereafter, he published the first of a number of books he's written—*UFOs: The Public Deceived*. Soon he was drawn into what became virtually a second full-time career in proving that what people *thought* were UFOs actually *all* had logical, natural explanations.

## Ice Crystals and Moonlight

An example was his response to the report of the pilot of a Japan Air 747 cargo plane, who said that he had encountered a giant UFO over Alaska. The incident occurred at a point when Klass was working sixteen-hour days. In addition to his responsibilities as a senior editor at *Aviation Week*, he had a book deadline bearing down upon him. But in order not to appear to be throwing in the towel as the dean of skeptics, Klass went to a twenty-hour day in order to come up with an answer.

His explanation on the Alaska sighting? After an intensive review of FAA reports, Klass deduced that, on the night of the sighting, there was a nearly full moon at approximately twelve degrees above the horizon, and the bright moonlight reflecting off turbulent clouds of ice crystals had generated the "undulating flame-colored lights" the pilot had seen.[7]

The role of "world's leading UFO skeptic" was not without its sacrifices. For Phil Klass it involved, in addition to the long hours of research, attendance at UFO conferences around the country, at which he was the proverbial "skunk at the garden party." He earned the animosity of rabid UFO believers, and had an almost lifelong lack of social outlet. (He did not marry until age sixty.)[8]

But Phil Klass was committed and on a crusade. He has been a most articulate spokesman for the skeptics.

## The Scientific Committee

A powerful ally for the debunkers came into existence in 1980 when the Committee for the Scientific Investigation of Claims of the Paranormal (CSICOP) was formed. Affiliated with the Council for Secular Humanism, CSICOP is a prestigious organization which publishes the respected journal *The Skeptical Inquirer*. Included in its fellows directorate are space scientists, psychologists, physicists, astronomers, biochemists and other science professionals.

The committee's 1996-1997 "Fund for the Future" campaign to raise "$20 million for the future of science and reason" was planned to enable a major expansion of the organization. Currently maintaining a Center for Inquiry (CFI) in Amherst, New York, adjacent to the University of Buffalo, CSICOP envisions a much greater role in public affairs in the years ahead.

Planned is a Council for Media Integrity, designed to monitor and refute media reports that CSICOP sees as unfounded or scientifically misleading; an expansion of the CFI Institute to offer a three-year certificate program in science and skepticism; enlargement of the "world's largest" CFI skeptic's library and its transition into electronic access, as well as a focus on the education of children in skepticism. The establishment of regional centers in the United States and greater liaison with affiliated international skeptics organizations is also underway.

Committed to the advancement of secular humanism, CSICOP is unquestionably a major player, not just on the UFO front (though it is definitely in that arena), but in a wide variety of places. CSICOP opposes all religions (except humanism), pseudo-science, creationism and every type of paranormal or supernatural phenomena.

A review of nearly a decade of *The Skeptical Inquirer* magazines reveals dozens of anti-UFO articles, all designed to show that the phenomenon is not real; that there are always logical explanations. Naturally, Phil Klass has been a frequent contributor.

One example among many of how *The Skeptical Inquirer* debunks UFO reports may be seen in the response to the records of the late nineteenth-century airship (UFO) sightings.

## 1896 Airships Debunked

In an extensive article entitled "The Airship Hysteria of 1896-97" by Robert Bartholomew in Volume 14, Winter 1990, the thesis is that, far from being sightings of UFOs, the airships were merely the fanciful perceptions of individuals with an "airship mind-set."

Bartholomew explains the numerous original airship reports in U.S. newspapers of the period (quoting T.E. Bullard, who has collected more than 1,000 separate airship-related newspaper stories from the 1890s), many of these witnessed by hundreds of persons at a time, in this way:

> In the presence of the widespread airship rumors holding that such an invention was on the verge of perfection, the ambiguity of the nighttime sky, and the intense emotions held by many Americans that such a dramatic achievement was at hand—and the fanning of these emotions by speculative and often fabricated newspaper stories—people attempted to relieve their emotionally aroused states by looking to the skies for proof or denial of the airship invention stories. They expected to see airships and they saw them. Whereas contemporary people collectively perceive "flying saucers" from outer space, citizens in 1896-97 were predisposed by the popular literature of the era to see airships.[9]

Bartholomew calls this the "autokinetic effect" which he says is the interpretation of ambiguous stimuli within a group setting which results in members developing an increased need to define the situation, depending less on their *own* judgment for reality validation and more on the judgment of *others*.

This, of course, is a hotly disputed conclusion.

"The Crop-Circle Phenomenon" in the Volume 16, Winter 1992 issue, is another example. This major nineteen-page article, abridged from a chapter in the book *Mysterious Realms*, explains away the worldwide appearances of elaborate crop circles and pictograms (flattened areas in grain fields that create these mysterious figures) as being the product of hoaxes by various individuals or groups.

Yet the article contains photos of immense pictograms which would require the enormous effort of a number of people (all done at night and without detection?). It closed with the statement, "The phenomenon is indeed mysterious, but the mystery may be only the ever-present one of human behavior."[10]

The Roswell "crash" has been the subject of numerous *Skeptical Inquirer* articles, among them "TV Movie on Roswell Incident" (January-February 1995, pp. 22-23); "The Roswell Incident and Project Mogul" (July-August 1995, pp. 15-18) and "The Roswell Fragment—Case Closed" (November-December 1996, pp. 5-6).

The bottom line, according to the writers, is that the debris recovered by Mac Brazel in 1947 was the remnant of a balloon flight launched as part of a top-secret program called Project Mogul, as revealed by documents obtained through the Access to Information Act and by the testimony of several of the individuals involved in the project.

Thus the whole story about the recovered crashed alien spacecraft with four bodies, as well as the purported film of the alien autopsy, is "thoroughly debunked."

Numerous other examples could be cited.

Obviously there are formidable opponents to the belief that UFOs are anything other than unusual natural occurrences—or hoaxes.

And yet, strangely enough, some of the very people who oppose the idea of UFOs are involved in a related search.

## Scientists Search for ETI

From an entirely different perspective than that of either the believers or the skeptics, another kind of ongoing research was launched in the early 1960s. SETI—the Search for Extraterrestrial Intelligence—is an attempt, through a continuous radio telescope scan of the universe, to discover if intelligent life exists somewhere in space.

Thus, on April 8, 1960, from a modest eighty-five-foot radio telescope in rural Green Bank, West Virginia, Project Osma began under the umbrella of NASA. It is mankind's most ambitious and costly attempt to make contact with extraterrestrials. After detecting, on the second day of operation, an apparent (but unsubstantiated) signal from outer space, the searchers' efforts to date (July 1997) have been fruitless.

Nevertheless, through the ups and downs of government funding and private financial support, SETI has continued at enormous cost. A 1996 fund-raising letter from The Planetary Society, founded in 1980 by Carl Sagan, Bruce Murray and Louis Friedman, gives some idea of the magnitude of the ongoing search. Friedman writes:

We may be best known for our support of SETI—the Search for Extraterrestrial Intelligence. We operate the largest *continuous* search in the world. Our Project BETA, working off a Harvard University radio telescope, scans a quarter of a billion radio channels simultaneously for possible signals from other civilizations. Meanwhile, our Project META at a site near Buenos Aires, Argentina, is the only continuous search occurring in the vital Southern Hemisphere, facing directly toward the galactic center. And recently, we added Project SERENDIP at the giant Arecibo Observatory in Puerto Rico.

Movie producer Steven Spielberg adds to the appeal by explaining:

Some scientists argue that as many as *100 million solar systems* in the Milky Way may harbor intelligent life. But reaching them is no small matter. The vast distances between stars, and the limitations on speed we face, mean neither we nor they will likely visit soon.

But with an inexpensive, efficient form of communication—radio waves—we CAN "visit" and aliens can "visit" us. Radio can allow us to trade the most important thing any civilization possesses: information.

The Planetary Society's Project BETA has transformed this idea from dream to logical, thoughtful, comprehensive search by probing the skies on a quarter of a billion radio frequencies. Soon, the Society will expand Project BETA to cover 6 *billion* radio channels.

It's safe to say that the Society now operates the most powerful continuous SETI detection system on Earth![11]

In spite of the fact that prominent Planetary Society member Spielberg produced the films *Close Encounters of the Third Kind* and *E.T.*, the Society members generally fall into the skeptical category when it comes to UFOs.

Among them is the late Carl Sagan, one of the society's co-founders. A truly distinguished and internationally recognized scientist, he believed passionately in the need for the promotion of science and gave himself unstintingly to it. A Pulitzer Prize winner, Dr. Sagan received the highest award of the National Academy of Sciences, the citation for which reads:

> No one has ever succeeded in conveying the wonder, excitement, and joy of science better than he . . . and few as well. His ability to capture the imagination of millions and to explain difficult concepts in understandable terms is a magnificent achievement.[12]

Sagan's ability to communicate his passion for

science, as well as his skepticism, is very forcefully detailed in his final book, *A Demon-Haunted World*. In it Sagan rejects the possibility of the supernatural and UFO paranormality.

In Sagan's view, the unseen supernatural world— God or gods, angels, demons, spirits—exists only in the minds of gullible unscientific people, though he does not use this specific term. For example, he explores the satanic ritual abuse phenomenon (the claim that many people have been tortured or murdered in secret occult rituals) and points out that not a single case has ever been proven. He presents a convincing argument.

Sagan also takes on New Agers, faith and psychic healers, astrologers, witches, psychics and other dabblers in the paranormal. He rejects creationism, dismissing it with virtually no examination—at least in this book.

The thesis of his final volume is that, at this crucial juncture of human history, it is essential that solutions come through a scientific approach.

His fear was that mankind, under the pressure of global problems, will revert to an irrational belief in the supernatural (particularly visitors from outer space) for solutions. Thus, Sagan envisioned the danger of "the candle of science being snuffed out by the darkness of irrationality."[13]

## UFO "Bashing"

And Sagan devotes a great deal of attention to the UFO phenomenon, concluding that "Essentially all the UFO cases [are] anecdotes, something

asserted." In support of that conclusion, this former member of Project Blue Book offers a good
deal of what he considers proof.

He lists several of the hoaxes, such as the 1992
crop circle "exposé" by Doug Brown and Dave
Chorley—two British "blokes" who reportedly
created them for fifteen years, as described in the
book *Round in Circles* by John Schnabel.

The Roswell crash is explained by the fact that
the secret Project Mogul was on at the time. The
crash debris was "that of a long-range, highly secret, balloon-borne, low-flying acoustic detection
system, designed to test Soviet nuclear weapons
explosions at sub-stratospheric altitudes."

The millions of UFO sightings are attributed
by Sagan to mistaken perceptions. He says, "Most
people honestly reported what they saw, but what
they saw was natural, if unfamiliar, phenomena."
In addition to the natural explanations offered by
other debunkers, Sagan lists things such as optical
mirages, effects of temperature inversions, radar
"angels"—something that seems to be there, but
isn't—small comets, satellites, nose cone reentries
and so on.

Then Sagan zeroes in on the UFO abduction
reports, arguing for logical explanations which
would indicate that such experiences occur only in
the minds of the abductees.

In suggesting such explanations, he deals at
length with false memory syndrome, in which
nonexistent childhood sexual abuse is "remembered"—often stimulated by unprofessional thera-

pists with hidden agendas. Such "memories," or sheer fantasy about the "abuses," is drawn out as "proof" of alien abduction.

Sagan also presents sleep paralysis—a medical condition—as another explanation for the abduction accounts. Sleep paralysis occurs in "the twilight world between being fully awake and fully asleep." Symptoms of sleep paralysis are immobility, anxiety, the sense of a weight on one's chest, quickened heartbeat, labored breathing, inability to cry out and auditory and/or visual hallucinations. Sagan quotes Robert Baker of the University of Kentucky as saying that sleep paralysis has "the full force and impact of reality." Car-trip abductions are explained by the "auto-hypnotic reverie."[14]

And yet, a brief questioning note creeps into this section. Sagan notes that a 1969 study by the National Academy of Sciences acknowledged that there are "numerous reports not easily explained."[15] He also observes that "absence of evidence is not evidence of absence"—an axiom which can cut both ways.

## The Unending Search for UFOs

Thus the *U.S. News and World Report* headlined a story on the fact that members of "legitimate UFO organizations" feared that the Heaven's Gate incident would hurt their efforts to prove the existence of extraterrestrials.

The article reported on the efforts of the Asheville, North Carolina-based Center for the

Study of Extraterrestrial Intelligence (CSETI) to present its evidence at a briefing in April 1997 for interested members of Congress. The event was cohosted by Apollo astronaut Ed Mitchell, with the aim of moving the UFO debate out of the tabloids and into public hearings. Photos, videos and the testimony of U.S. military intelligence and private-sector workers who claim to have seen UFO debris were features of the event.[16]

A renewed debate over the authenticity of the Roswell crash broke out on June 24, 1997, the eve of the fiftieth anniversary celebrations of that historic event.

It occurred when the USAF released *The Roswell Report: Case Closed*, a detailed 231-page explanation that the bodies recovered in the crash were not aliens, but rather dummies used in high-altitude parachute tests code-named High Dive and Excelsior. The *Report* was intended to "close the book" on long-standing rumors that the Air Force had recovered a flying saucer and extraterrestrial bodies in 1947 and had since engaged in a cover-up.

The publication inflamed, rather than ended, the debate. Skeptics immediately pointed out that the parachute tests were conducted from 1954-1959, at least seven years after the crash.

They also mocked the idea that the crash dummies, with an aluminum skeleton, skin of latex or plastic, cast aluminum head and instrument cavity in head and torso, could have been mistaken by witnesses for corpses of living beings.[17]

It was also pointed out that by acknowledging the reality of some kind of "bodies" at the crash site, the Air Force contradicted previous denials of *anything* being recovered. Consequently, the trust factor was dealt a further blow, and the polarization was deepened.

And so the debate rages and the polarization continues, deeper and more bitter than ever. And yet, in spite of the "heroic" efforts of the debunkers, the fact remains that the worldwide reports of UFO phenomena are so vast that at least half of the U.S. population concludes "There *has* to be something happening!"

Is there?

That's the question we'll explore in chapter 5, in which we'll also suggest what appears to be the logical conclusion.

Part Two

# *Scientific*
# *or*
# *Supernatural?*

If the sheer weight of evidence leads us to the assumption that *something* real is going on in the UFO phenomena, our next question logically is: What?

Are these truly unexplained, incredibly intriguing entities scientific or supernatural? That is, are they the product of remarkable intelligence—either human or extraterrestrial? Could they be, on the one hand, the result of secret projects by some earthbound government or military? On the other hand, is earth in fact being visited by superior beings from outer space?

Or are these mysterious objects and entities from some other dimension—namely, the supernatural?

Let's explore the options.

# CHAPTER FIVE

## *The Conclusion Is Apparent*

For anyone to suggest that he or she has discovered the truth about UFOs is to leave himself or herself open to a good deal of criticism—probably fairly well deserved.

As we have attempted to show in the previous chapter, the reports of UFO incidents and the opinions about them cover an extremely wide range of convictions. And that survey is, of necessity, very, very superficial given our space constraints.

The key issue, without doubt, is whether UFOs and encounters with them are real.

### There Are Logical Explanations, but . . .

Admittedly there are many natural and logical explanations for a very high percentage of UFO sightings and encounters. Astronomer Hugh Ross calculates, on the basis of over twenty years of UFO research, that more than half of reported UFO sightings are really the planet Venus. To people unfamiliar with astronomy, he explains, Venus could look very much like a UFO; it is a very bright planet and once every three years this early morning celestial body sheds enough radiance to enable one to read a newspaper by its light. Little wonder that skeptics have cited Venus as an explanation for a great many UFO sightings.

In Canada to the north, says Ross, the cluster Pleiades can be, and often is, mistaken for a group of UFOs.

*Venus and other planets* are only one of several common, natural explanations for UFOs which Dr. Ross cites. His listing includes:

*Meteors*, which can produce fireballs that may appear to be larger than the moon;

*Birds*, particularly plovers, that collect phosphorous dust in their feathers. Under certain conditions, they can appear as lighted objects performing erratic maneuvers in the sky;

*Inversion layers of clouds*, which are unusual cloud shapes that reflect light and appear to be objects in the sky. Numerous books contain photos which show how this natural phenomenon can resemble spacecraft;

*Experimental military aircraft*, the development of which is shrouded in secrecy. Examples of such aircraft that are now declassified include the "Flying Flapjack" and "The Flying Wing" of the 1950s and, more recently, the Stealth Bomber. Undoubtedly there are others that have yet to be made public, and those who have somehow observed such devices are convinced they've seen a UFO;

*Photos taken inside a window*, which may include a reflection of interior lights, giving the appearance of a UFO hovering in the air.[1]

Dr. Michael Persinger, professor of psychology at Laurentian University, Sudbury, Ontario, has documented the fact that reports of UFO sightings frequently increase prior to seismic events such as earthquakes. According to Persinger, the tectonic strain within the earth's crust creates short-lived luminosities (balls of light) which appear in the sky as UFOs.[2]

These and other natural explanations for UFOs account for an estimated ninety-five percent of all sightings.

## It's a Tough Task

And yet for all this, the debunkers and skeptics have a very difficult task before them in their efforts to disprove the existence of UFOs.

Granted, there have been, are and no doubt will be hoaxes galore—given human nature.

Agreed, there are natural explanations for millions of sightings.

Admittedly, there are bizarre beliefs and out-
landish claims about UFOs—in abundance.

But the fact remains that there have been multiplied millions of reported UFO incidents in countries around the globe. The comment of John
Ankerberg and John Weldon in *The Facts on UFOs*
is insightful:

> It is only by examining the history of the
> phenomenon since 1947, the recently declas-
> sified documents under the Freedom of In-
> formation Act, and the publications of
> leading civilian organizations in 20 countries
> around the world that we begin to compre-
> hend some of the magnitude of the phe-
> nomenon. It strains credulity to believe that
> organizations such as the CIA, State Depart-
> ment, National Security Agency, FBI,
> Army, Navy, Air Force, and Defense Intelli-
> gence Agency would spend decades and vast
> amounts of resources in studying a nonex-
> istent phenomenon.[3]

Nor should one lightly dismiss the experience
of J. Allen Hynek, who progressed from skeptic to
believer. Hynek had access to tremendous
amounts of information and research, first as a
Project Blue Book astronomer and later as director
of the Center for UFO Study. The wealth of
documentation convinced Hynek of the existence
of genuinely unexplained phenomena.

And what does one make of experiences like the

ones my two sets of friends had, as described at the beginning of the first chapter? They saw something real—something that defied description.

Or how does one explain the implications of the following letter to the editor, written by Peter A. Bostrom, of Troy, Illinois?

> Though I am not a UFO investigator, I still follow up on interesting stories if they seem important.
>
> The farm next to mine has, since 1991, had circles appear in a particular species of aquatic plant. When the phenomenon first appeared, my neighbors saw exotic flying objects directly over the area affected. The circles appear each year in June on the exact same spot. I've also found this to be happening in the same way on a site located 200 miles away in Missouri.
>
> My own investigations yielded no explanation. Aquatic plant specialists at Purdue University dismissed the matter, saying it is "like parapsychology." You would think some scientist would jump at the chance to study something as predictable as this. I could never find anyone to seriously study these phenomenon [sic].[4]

Or how can the statement of Dr. Edward Condon, chairman of the Condon Commission on UFOs, be brushed aside? Condon, a self-proclaimed skeptic, acknowledged in the commission's report that there were incidents that appeared to be real.

## The View of Scientists

When *Unmasking the Enemy* authors Nelson Pacheco and Tommy Blann mailed a question-naire on UFOs to 2,611 members of the American Astronomical Society, 1,356 responded—an astonishing return of over fifty percent, indicating a very high degree of interest. The survey revealed that fifty-three percent of the respondents felt, with varying degrees of intensity, that the UFO problem deserved scientific study. Only twenty percent had a negative response (most of these saying "*probably* not"), with the remainder not expressing themselves on the question (italics added).

If the survey respondents are typical, then a majority of astronomers feel there is suffecent real-ity in the UFO phenomenon to deserve further study. In fact, seventy-five percent indicated a de-sire for more information—but wanted it from scientific journals as opposed to lectures, books or the media.

Sixty-two respondents had witnessed or obtained an instrument record of an object they could not identify, which they believed might relate to the phenomenon. Only thirty percent of these had re-ported such observation to anyone in authority.[5]

## Strong Statements

Los Angeles-based reporter Stuart Goldman

concludes a research article with the following comment:

> [T]he unpleasant fact is, fifty thousand people cannot all be lying. Something is here— probing people, inspecting them, planting thoughts in their minds and manipulating their bodies—treating them, in a sense, like so many cattle.[6]

Dr. Jacques Vallee in *Revelations* forthrightly declares:

> There is a genuine UFO phenomenon and it is not explained by the revelations of alleged government agents . . . [or] by the cultists. . . .[7]
>
> In the first two volumes of this Alien Contact trilogy [*Dimensions* and *Confrontations*], I have shown that unidentified flying objects do exist. . . . They should be seriously and calmly investigated by the full power of science. . . .[8]
>
> Yet the UFO phenomenon is undeniably real. It is amazingly consistent and tantalizing, seductive and secret; always just a fraction of an inch beyond our reach.[9]

Vallee, frequently a very vocal critic and often a debunker of much of the popular UFO hysteria, nevertheless clearly believes that there is a genuine, worldwide UFO phenomenon which is supported by the testimony of thousands of reliable witnesses. He estimates that there have been at least 5,000 documented cases of "close encounters," a sizeable number observed at close range by multiple witnesses. In some instances there have been physical indications of landings—indentations in the ground, burnt grass, abnormal radiation levels and so on. He writes:

> I am among those who believe that UFOs are real. . . . UFOs, whatever they are, remain visible to the naked eye, are detectable by satellite, electronic sensors and radar.[10]

## Conclusion

The worldwide magnitude of the phenomenon; the numerous physical indicators (both in people and in the environment) of the presence of unexplained objects; the multiplied thousands of sightings by credible witnesses, often previously skeptical; the global research by bona fide scientists—all tend to point to one conclusion.

That conclusion seems to be apparent: UFOs are real!

The very conservative and generally accepted estimate is that at least five percent of UFO sightings simply cannot be explained. This means that, out of the millions of worldwide sightings and encounters, literally thousands are real, unexplained experiences.

It has been suggested that, in order for someone to state that UFOs do *not* exist requires that person to be omniscient—that is, possessing all knowledge. If a person admits that he does not know *everything*, he must also admit that, within the realm of the knowledge not possessed, UFOs could exist.

The evidence is that they do.

## In Light of This Conclusion . . .

If we accept that UFOs are real, the next question logically is: What are they?

Are they the product of advanced scientific knowledge, developed either by human or extraterrestrial intelligence? Or are they supernatural?

Chapter 6 considers these questions.

# CHAPTER SIX

# *Real—but Not Physical*

UFOs can do incredible things!

At one time or another in the past fifty years their unbelievable feats have been monitored on radar or sighted visually, often by multiple witnesses. An example is the NORAD radar trackings described in chapter 2, which involved dozens of radar stations all locked in on the same UFOs, performing impossible maneuvers.

UFOs can go instantly from a dead stop to speeds of up to 15,000 to 18,000 miles per hour.

They can be traveling at thousands of miles per hour and come suddenly to a complete stop: from 15,000 miles per hour to 0 miles per hour in an instant!

They can make sudden right-angle turns while traveling at thousands of miles per hour.

They can perform intricate maneuvers, defying belief, including appearing and disappearing suddenly. UFOs can plunge into an ocean or other large body of water and reemerge to continue their flight.

UFOs have been seen—often by a number of credible witnesses—doing not only the above, but also affecting the operation of vehicles and various other instruments. Other remarkable capabilities have been attributed to them as well, such as changing shape and color.

Are these incredible objects the product of scientific intelligence—human or extraterrestrial?

During World War II and through the late 1940s, as well as in the next few decades as the Cold War raged, the Nazis, the Russians, the U.S. and Britain, respectively, *all* feared that UFOs were secret military developments of the enemy.

But such is not the case. I submit that UFOs are not the product of human scientific knowledge.

## Not "Made on Earth"

That these amazing objects are not the product of human scientific expertise is the studied conclusion of a number of respected UFO researchers and scientists.

Former British Admiral of the Fleet, Lord Hill-Norton, G.C.B., in a foreword to Timothy Good's 1988 book *Above Top Secret: The Worldwide UFO Cover-Up*, writes:

> I must say that I simply do not believe [that UFOs are man-made by one or both of the superpowers]. If it were so, then I am sure that during my time as Chief of the Defense Staff I could not have failed to be let in on the secret, and I was not. . . . I am certain

that were such technology in actual use any-
where on earth it would have surfaced,
either in war or, perhaps more likely, in in-
dustry.[1]

Jacques Vallee is generally considered to be the
world's foremost scientist involved in UFO research. An astrophysicist, Vallee holds a Ph.D. in
computer science and has been a principal investi-
gator on Department of Defense computer projects. He became an associate of J. Allen Hynek
and a UFO researcher when Hynek left Project
Project Blue Book and began to independently investigate UFO phenomena. Vallee has since written a number of books detailing his research and
conclusions.

With such experience and credentials, Vallee's
opinions obviously carry a good deal of weight.

And in his book *Dimensions*, Vallee states his
opinion very clearly:

My interest in UFOs has gone through
several phases, but my curiosity has never
been satisfied about the behavior of scientists who destroy, distort or simply ignore
the very facts they should investigate. . . .
We have thousands of unexplained observations by reliable witnesses. . . . We have
come to realize that we are dealing with a
genuine new phenomena [sic] of immense
scope. *The UFOs are real* (italics added).[2]

Thornton Page, an astrophysicist with the NASA Johnson Space Center in Houston, offers his studied conclusion:

> The record of the past thirty years shows that some 95 percent of UFO reports can be explained, that 2 or 3 percent are frauds, but that the remaining 2 or 3 percent are reliable and truly unexplained.[3]

Hugh Ross is a respected scientist and astronomer who has served at observatories in British Columbia, Ontario and California. He is the founder and director of the organization Reasons to Believe. Dr. Ross, who has studied the UFO phenomenon for several decades also believes they are real, but has come to the conclusion that they are not physical.

In a TV lecture entitled UFOs: The Mystery Unraveled, Ross makes the following points, among others, to explain why he believes UFOs cannot possibly be physical.

- There's never a sonic boom from a UFO: never one heard or recorded by instrument. Whenever any physical object exceeds the speed of sound and breaks the sound barrier, there's always a sonic boom. Since there is never one with UFOs they are apparently not physical.
- A physical object must encounter air resistance when it exceeds certain velocities (as

does a spacecraft which heats up as it reenters the earth's atmosphere). UFOs do not manifest any evidence of air resistance in spite of their incredible speeds; therefore they cannot be physical.

- UFOs often project light beams which stop suddenly at a particular point. A physical beam of light cannot behave in this fashion, but rather must dissipate gradually.

- UFOs frequently violate the laws of physics. They make incredible right-angle turns and sudden starts or stops at thousands of miles per hour. A solid ball of steel could not survive the G-forces these maneuvers would create: their molecules would fly apart. Any physical craft or being subjected to such stress forces would be utterly destroyed.

- They change shape, size and color at random, appear, disappear, disintegrate and reassemble. Physical objects cannot do any of these things.

- UFOs fly in tight formation at incredible speeds without any evidence of electromagnetic communication or contact. It's physically impossible to do such things without communication.

- No physical artifact or crash debris has ever been recovered—in spite of the Roswell Crash stories.[4]

A roll call of scientists who have come to the same conclusion about UFOs could be called, but it's very obvious: UFOs are real, but not physical.

## Nor Are They Extraterrestrial

UFOs may be extraordinary, but they are not extraterrestrial.

It should be quite apparent that the physical limitations imposed on human beings also apply to extraterrestrials, as well as to any physical object—regardless of where it comes from. The laws of physics are universal.

But there are additional compelling reasons why UFOs cannot possibly be from other planets or galaxies. The two major reasons are, first, the unimaginable odds against the existence of a planet which could sustain life (despite the vast number of star systems "out there") and, second, the impossible distances and time involved in extraterrestrial or intergalactic travel. These very effectively and completely rule out such travel for any physical person or object.

Dr. Ross explains why.

> The nearest star to earth is Alpha Centauri, which is four-and-a-half light years away. That distance represents a 70,000-80,000 year-round trip to earth based on present technology. And Alpha Centauri is the only star within a "reasonable distance" (if 80,000 years is reasonable) from which to expect any kind of visitation. Any other star deemed capable of sustaining life would have to manifest some forty parameters (type of galaxy, location in that galaxy, age,

mass and so on)—like our sun. The possibility that such a star exists is believed by astronomers to be one chance in ten billion, with the distance from earth being almost incalculable.[5]

Ross points out that it is completely unreasonable to believe that there could be physical extraterrestrial visits to earth, based on current or foreseeable technology within the framework of the laws of physics.

He maintains that when we conclude that UFOs can function at velocities beyond the speed of light we can no longer classify them as physical. Conceding that extraterrestrials have found ways to violate the laws of physics "automatically defines the habitat of such entities as a realm transcending space and time, which in itself makes them spiritual beings for all practical purposes."[6]

The summary of Dr. Thornton Page of NASA is significant:

Over the last thirty years, many astronomers have agreed that there may be millions of other planets orbiting stars in the Milky Way Galaxy. A few of these may be like Earth and may have developed intelligent life such as humans. We expect them, like humans on Earth, to overpopulate their planets and seek to leave by spacecraft to colonize other planets. The numbers can be roughly summarized by noting that there

are about 100 billion stars in our galaxy; perhaps 10 percent of them—10 billion—have
planets, and maybe 1 percent of these planets have Earthlike conditions that can support life. It seeems reasonable that life would
develop on some fraction of the 100 million
Earthlike planets, so one could expect something like 10 million different homes for extraterrestrial life in our galaxy at distances
between 10,000 and 50,000 light years from
Earth. However, only the first of these numbers is well established. The fraction of stars
having planets rests on approximate *theories*
of star formation, *and the development of life on
other Earthlike planets is pure guess.*

The new line of reasoning is that if extraterrestrials are colonizing other planets
using spacecraft for interstellar flight, we
should detect them with our powerful radio
telescopes on Earth long before they get
here in their flying saucers and mother
ships. . . . *It seems that we humans ARE alone in
our galaxy* [italics added].[7]

So, what are UFOs?

To focus on the answer, let's diagram our con-
siderations to this point (see end of chapter).

UFOs can be only one of two possibilities: real
or not real. If we accept the general consensus of
respected investigators that they *are* real, there are
then only two possibilities: UFOs are either scientific (physical) or supernatural (nonphysical).

If we accept the premise that they are physical, there are only two possibilities: they are the product of either human or extraterrestrial intelligence.

Ruling out the possibility of UFOs being physical leaves only the possibility that they are supernatural, for these are the only choices. And if supernatural there are only two choices: they are either benevolent (angels) or malevolent (demons).

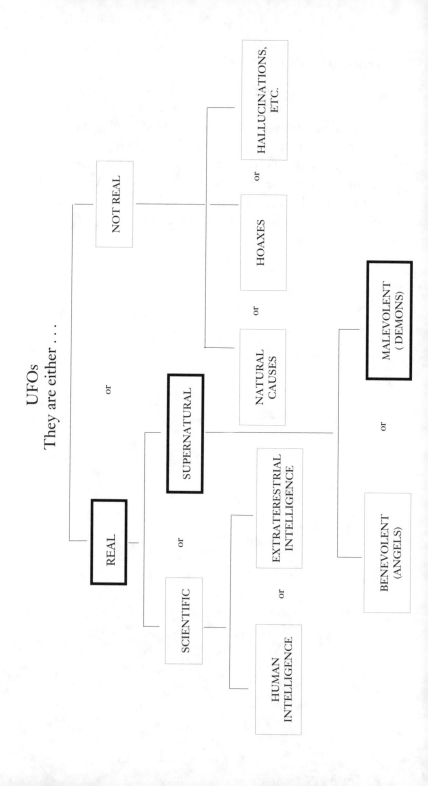

UFOs
They are either . . .

REAL

or

NOT REAL

SCIENTIFIC

or

SUPERNATURAL

HOAXES

or

HALLUCINATIONS,
ETC.

HUMAN
INTELLIGENCE

or

EXTRATERRESTRIAL
INTELLIGENCE

NATURAL
CAUSES

BENEVOLENT
(ANGELS)

or

MALEVOLENT
(DEMONS)

Part Three

# Friend
## or
## Foe?

If the assumption is accepted that UFOs are real, but not physical entities, and therefore are from a different dimension, another question is immediately raised.

What kind of supernatural beings are they? Are they good or evil spirit beings—angels or demons?

Are they benevolent—with mankind's best interests in view, or are they deceptive, malevolent beings bent on bringing harm and destruction to people?

UFO entities are said to profess great affection for humankind. They are reputed to be prepared, with their obviously superior knowledge, to provide guidance that will enable the human race to deal with the threats to our existence: environmental destruction and nuclear war.

In fact, in the messages being reported from UFOnauts, these entities reiterate a desire to lead humans into a coming new age of peace and plenty.

However, before we examine their character and their purported messages, we need to consider several issues relating to the spirit realm, which have a bearing on the entire UFO question.

CHAPTER SEVEN

# *Questions about Spirit Beings*

Without doubt, the existence and nature of the spirit realm is something about which there are numerous viewpoints and opinions. On the one hand are those, best represented by the late Carl Sagan, who deny the very existence of this dimension, relegating belief in it to the category of outmoded superstition. On the other hand, among those who accept the fact of the spiritual dimension—including many bona fide scientists—viewpoints vary and questions surface.

Our purpose is to consider just two questions which have a particular bearing on the subject of UFOs as spirit entities: First, how are spirit beings able to materialize? Second, how are they able to create physical effects upon people and the environment?

## Question #1:
## How Can Spirit Beings Materialize?

Materialization is best described as the unaccountable appearance and disappearance of non-material images and objects in material form.

The late Dr. Kurt Koch, widely considered during his lifetime to be the leading Christian authority on the paranormal, devotes a major section of his classic volume *Christian Counseling and Occultism* to the subject. He quotes Professor F. Gruber, from his book on psychical discoveries—*Zeitschrift fur Arbeit und Besinnug*—as saying,

> Telekinesis and materialization are scientific facts. Certain persons have . . . the ability to . . . create outside their bodies . . . some visible, tangible, more or less organized form, sometimes supplied with its own illumination, patterned in many cases on parts or the whole of the human body. These materializations can appear and disappear suddenly.[1]

Koch admits that manifestations can be, and unquestionably are, faked as the result of deception, superstition or hoax, but he argues that there are real manifestations. He suggests several ways that genuine appearances of spirit entities in visible form may be explained. In doing so, he discusses at length (far beyond the scope of this book) the following:

- The ability of the spirit world to produce teleplastic forms;
- The openness of matter to the fourth dimension—that is, to the nonphysical world;

- The proof from nuclear physics that matter, in its basic component—the atom—is simply energy, consisting of electrons orbiting a nucleus, with the space between the charges much greater than the mass of the charges. The nature of matter thus makes possible materialization.[2]

Dr. Nandor Fodor and Dr. Leslie Spence in *The Encyclopedia of Occultism and Parapsychology* discuss the mysterious fact, frequently demonstrated before witnesses and periodically photographed, of the ability of mediums (individuals with psychic capability) to apparently become a link between the spirit world and the physical world. Ectoplasmic apparitions are cited, as well as mediumistic communication through physical means such as rapping (knocking), table-turning or lifting and the levitation of objects and people.[3]

Fodor quotes Professor R. Richet in *Thirty Years of Psychical Research* who suggests that

materialization is a mechanical projection; we already know the projection of light, of heat and of electricity; it is not a very long step to think that a projection of mechanical energy may be possible. The remarkable demonstrations of Einstein show how close mechanical and luminous energy are to one another.[4]

Astronomer Hugh Ross postulates in his video lecture *UFOs: The Mystery Resolved* that materializations are forms of energy—which is what matter is, in its basic form. He claims that there is evidence for *energy* in physical phenomena generated by spirit beings, but no evidence for *matter*, as such.[5]

Dr. Robert O. Becher of the University of Kentucky, a physician who is widely known for his work on the biological effects of electromagnetism, extends his work to subsume psychic phenomena in general. He says:

> Scientific discoveries of the past three decades have gradually resulted in a new paradigm of the nature of life. . . . This intimate relationship between earth's geomagnetic field and living organisms stimulated a re-evaluation of the relationship between electromagnetic fields and psychic phenomena [read materializations] . . . [and showed that] a firm link has been established between them.[6]

Kurt Wagner, a physicist who earned his Ph.D. in the field of general relativity theory, comments:

> It seems to me likely that UFOs are large-scale violations of the second law [of relativity] in which energy is arranged to take on enough of a force field appearance so that it appears to look like matter, yet it's really just an energy concentration—it's not really solid matter in the usual sense.[7]

Parapsychologist George N.M. Tyrell, a former president of the Society for Psychical Research, discusses "apparitions" in his text by that title. He writes:

> In whatever sense the central [apparition] is "there," the auxiliary objects, the additional figures are "there" too. . . . Apparitional dramas need no more be confined to the portrayal of a single figure than need a cinematographic film. The situation is a rather strange one because, although nothing is *physically* present in space, something (a *visual* solid) is *visibly* present in physical space.[8]

That angels—the messengers of God—appear in human form is a fact so well documented by the experiences of multiplied thousands of people that it needs no proof here.[9]

The bottom line is that spirit beings can and do materialize—appear in visible form. Unquestionably, however, the subject is full of mystery. And the related question of how spirit beings can produce physical effects on people and the environment is also an intriguing one.

## Question #2:
## How Can Spirit Beings Produce Physical Effects?

Understandably and legitimately skeptics do ask: If UFOs and their supernatural entities are nonphysical, how do they create physical effects?

Abductees report scars, bruises, swellings and numerous other physical symptoms. How can this be, if in fact the beings are spiritual?

Perhaps a dramatic personal experience will be helpful here.

Beginning in the fall of 1973 and continuing for almost a year, my wife and I, along with an evangelist and his wife and a small group of people from the church I was serving, were involved in helping a deeply demonized person come to freedom. This individual, originally from Europe, had a very long family history of witchcraft and occult involvement, and was invaded by the counter-kingdom.

In the course of those months leading to the person's salvation and complete deliverance, we personally had experiences such as I had only read about before. We saw the materialization and dematerialization of several things, like a knife (witnessed by four persons); heard various personalities with different voices speak out of the afflicted person; and saw scratches appear suddenly and spontaneously on the individual's body.

Telephone conversations were frequently interrupted by weird voices and bizarre noises, with broken connections invariably resulting. The demonized person often could not be located by family or friends and had extensive periods of "missing time." At one point there was a hospitalization of several weeks' duration with a mysterious ailment which puzzled the doctors.

Suicidal thoughts, periodic irrational behavior

QUESTIONS ABOUT SPIRIT BEINGS

and times of depression or intense fear were often
experienced. It hurt to see the pain and misery of
this victim of demonic invasion.

On the other hand, the tremendous personality
change when the last of the demonic entities was
finally expelled was truly remarkable and a great
joy to see. All of the above was personally verified
by a number of witnesses.

Our involvement in exorcism up to that point,
and since, has been minimal. Perhaps, had we better known how to confront the enemy, we could
have seen deliverance come much more quickly.
But perhaps not. Our evangelist friend felt that
this case was the most difficult he had ever encountered.

Though the experience occurred almost
twenty-five years ago, it has left an indelible impression on me. I will never forget the amazing
demonstrations of demonic reality and power. But
much more significantly I remember the far
greater power and authority of the Lord Jesus
Christ, for which I am eternally grateful.

And as, in the course of writing this book, I
have researched the effects of UFO encounters on
contactees and abductees, I have been impressed
again and again by the similarity of their experiences with those of the demonized person whom
we had the privilege of helping years ago. I will
explore this similarity further in the next chapter.

I clearly recall seeing the physical effects caused
by demonic, that is nonphysical, forces. These included, as indicated earlier, the materialization of

objects and the inflicting of injuries—all witnessed simultaneously by no less than four persons.

I cannot explain it. But I've personally seen it. I know it is real.

## More Corroboration

The late Kurt Koch saw it as well, to a far greater extent than I. Dr. Koch, whom we quoted earlier, was recognized as the world's foremost Christian authority on the demonic. Over the years of his worldwide ministry, he dealt with hundreds upon hundreds of persons who had suffered demonic invasion. His carefully detailed and documented case studies in his texts on the subject reveal the sort of things we personally experienced.

There is unquestionably abundant evidence for the existence of the "parallel world" as Jacques Vallee (an agnostic) calls it, as well as adequate evidence for the capability of that world to impact ours. In his book *Revelations*, Vallee quotes from a series of letters written by well-known author Philip K. Dick. In them, Dick describes his personal encounters with an entity which first manifested by keeping him awake at night by "violent phosphene activity" (February 10, 1978).

The entity communicated within his head in the form of a "computer-like or AI-system-like voice."

Dick thought the entity was "an ionized, atmospheric, electrical life-form able to travel through time and space at will." His experience "during

the days following the imposition-
right word—the imposition of anoth'
onto mine, produced startling modi'
behavior" (February 20, 1978).

Dick wrote some 500,000 words of notes over a
four-year period concerning his "paranormal" experiences and concluded that:

> I will never really know what did in fact
> happen. Some living, highly intelligent en-
> tity manifested itself inside me and around
> me, but what it was, what its purpose was,
> where it came from—I have tried a thou-
> sand theories, and all work equally well, but
> at the same time each theory leaves some da-
> tum unexplained . . . and *I know this is not go-
> ing to change.* [Dick's emphasis.] I have the
> impression that a master game player and
> magician and trickster is involved (February
> 23, 1978).[10]

## Angel Appearances

Scores of books on angels have been written
recently, describing their frequent documented
appearances in human form to numerous people.
The Bible also provides the record of such occurrences. To list but a few, we note the accounts of:

- Abraham, who had a visit from several angels
  who foretold the birth of his son;

- Lot, who was rescued from Sodom by two angelic beings;
- General Joshua, who was commissioned by an angel of the Lord;
- Daniel, who was protected by an angel sent to shut the mouths of lions.

The Christmas angels who announced the birth of the Lord Jesus Christ are well known, as is the Easter angel, who declared His resurrection from the dead. There were several angelic visits in the early Church, such as the one which resulted in the deliverance from prison of the Apostle Peter—a deliverance which included the opening of locked doors, without keys, upon command.

There is no reason to doubt that, just as the obedient angels—the messengers of God—can appear in visible form, the dark, fallen angels—the demons—can do so as well.

## UFOs and Physical Effects

The UFO literature is full of examples of physical effects caused by UFOs. John Ankerberg and John Weldon cite case after case of documented instances of people who have been physically injured or even killed by UFO contact. Many examples of physical effects in the environment are cited as well.[11]

Do these cases rule out the possibility that UFOs have a demonic origin? Not at all. Spirit beings *can* create physical effects.

Pacheco and Blann cite the appearance of markings on persons' bodies:

> Such mysterious-looking . . . marks, often called the "devil's mark," have been noted in demonology cases over the years. A much-celebrated case of this occured to a boy in Mount Rainier, Maryland, in 1949. This case was to become the basis for the dramatized Hollywood production "The Exorcist." According to Thomas Allen, who wrote about the actual account which inspired the movie, "The scratches looked like the kind a cat makes, long and shallow, the marks of claws. They appeared on [the boy's] arms, legs and chest. Some seemed to form letters of the alphabet."[12]

A somewhat related phenomenon, inasmuch as it involves physical effects without visible cause, is the phenomenon of stigmatism. This is the term applied to the appearance, in people's bodies, of some of the kinds of wounds which Christ suffered on the cross—in hands, feet, forehead and back, as though caused by nails, thorns or whips. While some of the more than 400 stigmatics who have lived over the past 800 years have undoubtedly been fraudulent or legendary, many have been observed to have stigmata occur under strictly controlled conditions which preclude fraud and defy explanation.

The experience of stigmatic Giorgio Bongiovanni,

a "man who stands astride the worlds of ufology and religious phenomena," is intriguing. An article by Bob Rickard explains why:

> Bongiovanni, an Italian, claims to have received his stigmata during a pilgrimage to Fatima in 1989. His wounds—in hands, feet, side and forehead—have since bled daily. A cult, which runs a local school, has sprung up around him.
>
> What makes Bongiovanni's story even more remarkable is that he claims to have frequent visions of Jesus and Mary, His mother, who arrive in or descend from UFOs. He sees many UFOs, but for him there is no incompatibility between them and his religious visions, since he believes the ETs are "beings of light." They are, he says, angels—composed of "spiritual energy"—who speak to him telepathically. He has also met the traditional Grey aliens, whom he says are not demonic, but are from a civilization about 100 years ahead of us technologically. Doctors who have examined Giorgio's stigmata have reportedly been astonished, both at the rapidity with which the fresh blood coagulates (about 10 seconds), the absence of infection (as would be expected from any such large wound open for some time) and Bongiovanni's lack of anemia.
>
> Bongiovanni is increasingly seen at UFO

and related conventions. The stigmatic speaks freely of many unusual things: how he is the incarnation of Francesco Marto (one of the original child visionaries of Fatima); how the "beings of light" make the "genuine" crop circles, and that Jesus himself will return to earth at the end of this century "or in the first years of the next."[13]

And so, though mysterious and mystifying, I contend that spirit beings—demons—*can* appear in visible form and *can* inflict physical harm upon people.

And I believe that, increasingly today, the form taken by the dark fallen angels—demons intent on harming mankind—is as UFOnauts, who claim to have a helpful message for us earthlings, but who are, in reality, determined to destroy us.

I will detail in the next chapter why I make such a statement.

# CHAPTER EIGHT

# The UFOnauts in Profile

My purpose in this chapter is to show that UFO entities are demonic. It's not a politically correct position to take and leaves one open to ridicule from some quarters, but it is my considered viewpoint.

I agree with Brooks Alexander of the Spiritual Counterfeits Project who writes in the *SCP Journal*:

> Understandably, the "demonic option" has not been popular outside of the fundamentalist ghetto. There are several reasons for that. The most obvious reason is that among today's intellectuals, the biblical faith and worldview are not just marginalized, they are actively mocked and ridiculed. . . . Intellectual intimidation prevents most people from even exploring those avenues of thought.
>
> But there are other motives for dismissing the demonic option. One of them is the fact

that the implications of such ideas are larger than most of us want to deal with. A case in point is J. Allen Hynek, one of Vallee's colleagues in ufology. He briefly discusses a "spiritual" theory of UFOs but tiptoes away from it, almost fearfully, *because it explains too much*. According to Hynek, it opens up ". . . another can of worms. Then the problem is essentially solved; that explains why UFOs can make right-angle turns, that explains why they can be dematerialized, why sometimes they are picked up on radar and sometimes not, and why they are not detected by our infrared equipment. All that. But that's dangerous territory to tread."[1] [My emphasis.]

I am prepared to "tread the dangerous territory," for I am quite convinced that the evidence reveals UFOs to be demonic. Before presenting the reasons which have led me to this conclusion, however, I want to cite a few of the many prominent researchers who have also come to the same conclusion.

## Researchers Conclude They're Demonic

Lynne E. Catoe was the senior bibliographer for the 1969 U.S. Air Force Office of Scientific Research publication *UFOs and Related Subjects: An Annotated Bibliography*. This 400-page volume listed over 1,600 books and articles. Catoe required two full years to read through the thousands of pieces of literature and books surveyed for the bibliography. In her preface she makes this observation:

A large part of the available UFO literature is closely linked with mysticism and the meta-physical. It deals with subjects like mental telepathy, automatic writing and invisible entities as well as phenomena like poltergeist [ghost] manifestations and "possession." Many of the UFO reports now being published in the popular press recount alleged incidents that are *strikingly similar to demonic possession and psychic phenomena.*[2] [My emphasis.]

John Keel is acknowledged to be one of the world's best-informed researchers of the UFO phenomenon. He is the author of a number of books, including *The Mothman Prophecies* and *The Eighth Tower*. Keel, who is an agnostic, makes this statement in his classic volume *UFOs: Operation Trojan Horse:*

The UFO manifestations seem to be, by and large, merely minor variations of the age-old demonological phenomenon.[3]

Keel is quoted by Ross as saying,

Demonology is not just another "crackpo-tology." It is the ancient and scholarly study of monsters and demons who have seem-ingly coexisted with man throughout human history. Thousands of books have been writ-ten on the subject, many of them authored by educated clergymen, scientists and schol-ars. And uncounted numbers of well-docu-

mented demonic events are readily available
to every researcher. The manifestations and
occurrences described in this imposing literature are similar, if not entirely identical,
to the UFO phenomenon itself.[4]

John Ankerberg and John Weldon, in the conclusion to their excellent booklet *Facts on UFOs and
Other Supernatural Phenomena* say,

[UFO's] "earth" orientation historically,
and the fact that all UFO phenomena are
consistent with the demonic theory, indicate
that this explanation is the best possible answer for the solution to the UFO mystery.[5]

In the same booklet the authors say that space
did not permit their citing a large variety of illus-
trations from actual UFO encounters documenting the demonic nature of these contacts—but the
number of encounters is vast, with hundreds of
examples to be found in the pages of *The Flying
Saucer Review*, 1955 to 1995.

David Hunt, a prolific Christian author, states
in "The Cult Explosion," a 1980 tract, that

UFOs . . . are clearly not physical and seem
to be demonic manifestations from another
dimension, calculated to alter man's way of
thinking.[6]

Pierre Guerin, a UFO researcher and a scientist

associated with the French National Council for Scientific Research says, "The modern UFOnauts and the demons of past days are probably identical."[7]

Ankerberg and Weldon cite Stuart Goldman, a Los Angeles-based journalist who has investigated UFOs as a skeptic, including interviews with Whitley Strieber, author of the mega-best-sellers about his UFO abductions.

Goldman quotes Elaine Morganelli (one of the guests at a Strieber meeting) whose "simple yet chilling" conclusion is that Strieber is being contacted "not by friendly visitors, but by demons." He comments:

> One could write Morganelli off as some sort of Christian fanatic. However, she's not the only one who's come to the conclusion that Strieber's visitors—and in turn the beings who are abducting countless thousands of people—are nothing more that good old-fashioned demons, doing what they do best: stealing souls.[8]

## USAF Officers Agree

An intriguing book, self-published in 1994 by two former Air Force officers in an effort to "get out the truth [about UFOs]," has a definite bearing on the UFO/demonic connection. USAF Lieutenant Colonel (retired) Nelson Pacheco and Civil Air Patrol Second Lieutenant Tommy Blann met on-line and subsequently became coauthors of *Unmasking the Enemy*, a book which contends that demons portray themselves as extraterrestrials in order to be accepted, even welcomed, by humans.

"We are dealing with highly intelligent beings," says Pacheco, "and in their efforts to subvert us, they will use whatever cover they can."[9]

Pacheco, a Roman Catholic, and Blann, a Protestant, did not reach their conclusion on the basis of their religious beliefs, but rather after decades of studying such phenomena as crop circles, apparitions of the Virgin Mary, mutilated cattle, abductions and so on.

In an article by Patrick Huyghe in the October 1994 issue of *OMNI* magazine, Pacheco is quoted as saying, "We have no ulterior motive—not fame or money. We just want to get the truth out. If anything, it's been a risk to our professional reputations."[10]

In Dr. Pacheco's case, particularly, that reputation is considerable. During his twenty-one years in the Air Force he helped target Minuteman ballistic missiles and track satellites for the North American Aerospace Defense Command. Prior to his retirement in 1987 he was chairman of the mathematics department at the Air Force Academy.

How did the men come to their demonic theory on UFOs?

The first clue, they say, came from the hundreds of credible witnesses who have described these craft as simply "vanishing on the spot." Despite this ghost-like behavior, they add, the so-called craft still sometimes have physical effects, like tracking on radar, or leaving scars on abductees. For Pacheco and Blann these tangible clues meant UFOs could not be a manifestation of imagination alone.

"So we came to think that the phenomenon must be preternatural," says Pacheco, "which means something not of our world but interacting with it. And that, of course, is very close to the area of traditional religion. It is our belief that what we are seeing conforms very definitely with orthodox religious teaching on demonic angels."

In fact, say the duo, the evil nature of much UFO phenomena is devilishly obvious. "I don't know how anyone can study UFO abductions and still have doubts about whether what's happening is good or evil," Pacheco adds, citing the aliens' disregard of human free will. "When these beings discuss God, they set themselves up as the true saviors of humankind in order to undermine traditional Christianity."[11]

Numerous other researchers could be cited, but let's move now to a consideration of the reasons which detail why we hold the view that UFOs are demonic. To do so I propose to examine what has been learned about the UFOnauts in terms of their character, activities, effect on people, messages and the timing of their recent dramatically increased presence on our globe.

## Why Believe That UFOs Are Demonic?

### *Reason #1: Their Character*

The best words to use in describing the character of the UFO entities who have manifested themselves to people would have to be "contradictory" and "deceptive."

On the one hand they claim to desire the well-being of mankind, expressing eagerness to show us mortals how to avoid nuclear war, environmental disaster or other dangers. Their supposed vastly superior intelligence and technological know-how are to be made available for our benefit to lead us into a peaceful new "golden age" for Planet Earth. They're *benevolent* beings, we're told.

On the other hand these entities manifest malevolent characteristics. They "take" people against their will; they murder, rape and conduct physically invasive experiments and examinations on their abductees. They damage property and strike fear into those whom they visit.

These and similar stories from contactees are legendary, appearing over and over again in the UFO literature. The comment of an unidentified writer quoted in *UFOs: The Continuing Enigma* is insightful:

> How come in the 1950s the aliens were so different, being jolly spacemen with kooky

names and a desire to protect the human race from disaster? Why have they become obsessed with sexual and genetic issues?[12]

Whitley Strieber, whose three best-sellers, *Communion*, *Transformation* and *Breakthrough*, are the account of his ongoing abduction experiences, gives descriptions of his UFO visitors that are very revealing:

> I became entirely given over to extreme dread. The fear was so powerful that it seemed to make my personality evaporate. . . . "Whitley" ceased to exist. What was left was a body and a state of raw fear so great that it swept about me like a thick, suffocating curtain, turning paralysis into a condition that seemed close to death. . . . I died, and a wild animal appeared in my place. . . .
>
> I felt an absolutely indescribable sense of menace. . . . Whatever was there seemed so monstrously ugly, so filthy and dark and sinister. Of course they were demons. They had to be. And they were here and I couldn't get away. . . .
>
> [The visitors] were so terrible, so ugly, so fierce, and I was so small and helpless. I could smell that odor of theirs like greasy smoke hanging in my nostrils.[13]

Characteristics such as the above may be most fittingly applied to demonic entities.

## *Reason #2: Their Activities*

Character is expressed in actions. And, according to contactees and abductees, the UFOnauts are certainly not benign, judging by their activities.

UFO entities have been responsible for deaths, the abduction of unwilling victims, the rape of many, the invasive physical examination of others, scarring and bruising, fear, depression, illnesses and suicidal tendencies. Psychological damage has included sleep disturbances, phobias, panic disorders, obsessions, bizarre memories and psychosexual developmental problems. Property has been damaged, families disrupted and general havoc created in the lives of numerous individuals as a result of UFO encounters.

In the article "Abductions and the ET Hypothesis," psychologist David M. Jacobs writes:

> Physically, the abduction experience can leave its victims with a wide range of after-effects. Scars, eye problems, muscle pains, bruises, unusual vaginal and navel discharges, genital disorders, neurological problems, pregnancy anomalies, ovarian difficulties and so forth, are just a few of the myriad of physical problems associated with abduction experiences. Physical problems can have permanent and deleterious effects on abductees. They can seriously harm a person and significantly alter the course of one's life. Al-

though the physical effects of abductions can be extremely severe . . . [it is the psychological] problems that have the most destructive effect on the course of people's lives and on their relationships with others.[14]

Demons, universally recognized as the enemies of mankind, are the only spirit beings whose activities would parallel the above.

## Reason #3: Their Effect on People

Without doubt, this reason is one of the most significant and constitutes, in my judgment, perhaps the greatest proof of the demonic identity of the UFO entities.

In a word, the effect which UFOnauts have on people is virtually identical to that of demonic invaders, as a comparison of these conditions dramatically demonstrates. In reviewing these effects there will be an unavoidable slight overlap with some of the factors already considered in the two previous sections.

## The Occult Subjection Syndrome

K. Neill Foster, in his unpublished doctoral dissertation *Discernment, the Powers and Spirit-Speaking*, has identified what he calls The Occult Subjection Syndrome (OSS). Foster uses the term to describe the symptoms of major or minor satanic intrusion into the life of an individual.[15]

Foster has surveyed the writings and recorded lectures of a number of recognized researchers and leaders in the area of exorcism and the confrontation of demonization in individuals. His purpose was to ascertain the indicators of demonic invasion cited by each of these authorities. Accordingly, the summations of Kurt Koch, Ernest B. Rockstead, Mark I. Bubeck, Conrad Murrell, L. David Mitchell and others were tabulated.

The resulting compilation was condensed into ten key criteria to which Foster applied the OSS designation: terrorizing fear; unbelief and aversion to divine things; obsessive sexual problems; pseudo-charismata, heresies and other religious aberrations; compulsive behavior; ancestral occult bondage; inexplicable illnesses; suicidal or murderous intent; spiritism, clairvoyance, witchcraft; and inner voices.[16]

Foster's list is, of course, not a complete catalog of the symptoms of demonic invasion or possession. Others include a distinctive smell in conjunction with occult activities, uncontrollable rage, intense depression, disrupted sleep patterns, personality alterations and so on. Foster has simply listed the "top ten" found in his survey.

To compare the post-abduction symptoms of people who claim to have encountered UFOs with OSS is extremely enlightening.

A significant compilation of abductee symptoms has been developed from the case histories and experiences (most of these given in great detail) of a number of abductees as described in published material. Surveyed were *Abduction* by John Mack; *Encounters* by Edith Fiore; *The Omega*

*Project* by Kenneth Ring; *Alien Abductions, UFOs and the Conference at M.I.T.* by C.D.B. Bryan; *The Evidence for Alien Abductions* by John Rimmer; *Intruders* and *Missing Time* by Budd Hopkins; *Into the Fringe: A True Story of Alien Abduction* by Karla Turner; *Secret Vows: Our Lives with Extraterrestrials* by Denise Rieb Twiggs and Bert Twiggs; *Aliens Among Us* by Ruth Montgomery; *Testing the Spirits* by Elizabeth Hilstrom; *Dimensions: A Casebook of Alien Contact* by Jacques Vallee; *Alternate Perceptions: A Journal of UFOs, History, Native Spirituality and Paranormal Phenomena* Issue 37, Winter 1997; and Whitley Strieber's three abduction books: *Communion, Transformation* and *Breakthrough.*

While the books and journals listed above are only a fraction of those which could have been consulted, it is nevertheless fair to say that this short list includes the generally accepted major works on the subject. Furthermore, it is apparent that multiplying the number of case histories studied would have simply been corroboration of a clearly established pattern.

To be evenhanded, it is important to note that various studies have called into question the validity of some of the methods used to obtain information on the experiences of reported UFO abductees. For example, the methods and data of Harvard psychologist John Mack, who utilizes hypnotic regression and an analysis of the interviewee's breath, were denounced by some in the Harvard faculty, by members of the False Memory Syndrome Foundation and by science writer James Gleick as "anti-science." They were just as strongly defended by other professionals, including psychotherapists and contactees in the San Francisco Bay area, who were interviewed by writer Michael Miley and who supported Mack's findings.[17]

Unquestionably, debate over the validity of memories recovered through hypnosis is extensive and sometimes bitter. Budd Hopkins, in *Missing Time*, his book on abductees, includes a section of notes on hypnosis, in which he cites a number of news reports and science articles concerning the use by police of hypnosis as a valid tool, accepted in the courts.[18]

On the other hand, Martin T. Orne, a leading authority on hypnosis and director of experimental psychiatry at the Institute of Pennsylvania Hospital, concludes that hypnosis is an unreliable tool for establishing what has actually happened in the past. Orne's extensive research leads him to state that there is no way even an experienced hypnotist can tell what is true and what is invented in accounts elicited from persons under hypnosis. Particularly suspect, says Orne, is testimony obtained by hypnotists with pro-UFO views.[19]

An article in the January 18, 1997 issue of *The Economist* also calls into serious question the related theory that memories of childhood abuse are repressed and can be "recovered" in later life with the help of a therapist (sometimes using hypnosis).

The article concludes that "the weight of evidence is turning sharply against the theory."[20]

However, what cannot be disputed is the fact that people who claim to have been abducted do manifest certain symptoms, and that prior to their "abductions" had a degree of involvement with the occult, as we shall note in more detail later.

The compiled list of abductee symptoms, extrapolated from the above sources, bears a most significant resemblance to OSS. Included in the list are the following symptoms which appear most often—some of them in almost every case surveyed: fear, including terrorizing panic; sexual problems; physical difficulties and unexplained illnesses; suicidal tendencies; increased openness to the psychic/occult realm; continued communication, psychically, with UFO entities who are often extremely controlling; irrational behavior; and the promotion of aberrant religious views.

Again, there are numerous other symptoms recorded—"loss" of time; the recollection of distinctive odors; disruption of personal and family life and many more—though not to the extent of those listed above.

## The Similarity Is Striking

Note the remarkable similarity when the characteristics of OSS and the major post-abduction symptoms are charted side by side:

| OCCULT SUBJECTION SYNDROME | POST-ABDUCTION SYNDROME |
|---|---|
| Terrorizing fear | Fear, including terrorizing panic |
| Unbelief and aversion to divine things | Promotion of aberrant religious views |
| Obsessive sexual problems | Sexual problems |
| Pseudo-charismata, heresies and other religious aberrations | Promotion of aberrant religious views |
| Compulsive behavior | Irrational behavior |
| Ancestral occult bondage | Increased openness to psychic/occult realm |
| Inexplicable illness | Physical difficulties and unexplained illness |
| Suicidal or murderous intent | Suicidal tendencies |
| Spiritism, clairvoyance, witchcraft | Continued communication, psychically, with UFO entities |
| Inner voices | Continued psychic communication |

It is instructive to note also that Pacheco and Blann in *Unmasking the Enemy* have charted a total of several dozen symptoms which are either identical or very similar in both UFO contactees and demonized persons. Their chart, which is divided into the categories of apparitions, levitation, teleportation, kinetics, healings, communication and "superiors" (referring to a hierarchy of beings), demonstrates most convincingly the overlap of symptoms between the two sets of phenomena.[21]

## There's More Evidence

The obvious conclusion to be drawn from the above is that the demonic invasion of an individual and UFO abduction are synonymous. Consider a number of corroborating experiences and studies.

Various colored balls of light, sometimes reddish-orange to orange, and other strange lights along with paranormal events have often been reported in UFO and occult literature over the years. It is common knowledge among some Christian missionaries and veteran ufologists that in certain areas where the occult has a strong foothold, where ancient pagan sites are located, or where ritualistic ceremonies are performed, UFO and other paranormal manifestations are frequently reported. Eileen Buckle, a British ufologist, said that "It is probably no coincidence that in Brazil, where UFO reports have been numerous, spiritualism has a strong footing." Well-known theologian Kurt Koch has said, "The explanation that these UFO beings are to be thought of as materialized demons has the most justification. The mass of evidence for this is overwhelming. . . . UFOs appear most frequently in countries where the cult of Satan flourishes. UFOs and occult practices run parallel. It is clear that they have the same origin."[22]

Kenneth Ring is professor of psychology at the University of Connecticut, and considered one of the world's chief authorities on near-death experiences (NDE). In his book *The Omega Project: Near-Death Experiences, UFO Encounters and the Mind at Large*, Ring makes an exceptionally strong case for the link between NDEs and UFO encounters. "The Inner Dimensions of Alien Encounters," Michael Miley's article in the March/April 1997 issue of *UFO Magazine*, also takes note of the UFO/NDE/Out of Body Experience connection. He writes:

> Ring's NDE subjects showed similar psychophysical changes to those that Mack [a Harvard psychiatrist and author of *Abduction*] has subsequently reported in his UFO/alien contactees: a deepening spiritual awareness, loss of the fear of death, increased sensitivity to ecological concerns, the emergence of psychic and healing abilities, and a general change of life, oriented more toward knowledge and compassion.[23]

These studies are significant because they are yet other indications that UFO encounters parallel occult activities such as astral travel and near-death experiences. While a consideration of NDEs is beyond the scope of this book, John Ankerberg in his *The Facts on Near-Death Experiences*, among others, has clearly documented the characteristically occult nature of the NDE.[24]

Since NDEs and UFO experiences are so very much alike, as Ring has documented, the inference is clear: both are occultic.

To provide documentation of the harmful physical effects of UFO encounters, Jacques Vallee relates in *Confrontations* how he has personally investigated firsthand almost fifty cases of UFO contact. Vallee's meetings with the contactees usually took place on site—in Brazil, France and Argentina as well as the United States. More than simply negative physical effects, Vallee reports that while "many of the cases involve secondary physical and medical effects, twelve were cases of fatal injuries in which the victim typically succumbed within 24 hours."[25]

## A Shamanistic Event

Medicine Grizzlybear Lake is a Native American author who had a "shamanistic UFO encounter" in March 1975 on a "sacred mountain" in California. Lake says that in the encounter he was taken aboard a UFO for a trip, during which he received prophecies and instructions from entities whom he calls "ancient ancestral spirits."

Lake made public the experience and the prophecies—which were first published in 1975 in the New Age magazine *Psychic Times* (Eureka, CA) d later in two local newspapers in 1976, 1978 and 1985.

The prophecies, predictions and earth warnings were also given to numerous Native American tribal councils and urban Indian centers and were sent to Presidents Carter, Reagan and Clinton.

Lake claims that the publication of his UFO encounter and the resulting stress brought him public scorn (even from some of his Native brethren), eventual loss of his position as a professor at a California college, the break-up of his marriage, sickness and destitution. He credits the efforts of Indian elders and medicine men, using "the old methods," for his healing and restoration.

Twenty-six specific prophecies were given in this 1975 "shamanistic UFO event"—an experience that unquestionably has occultic overtones.

It is intriguing to note that some of Lake's predictions appear to have been accurate. These include prophecies of increasingly serious flooding in various parts of the U.S.; noticeable changes in worldwide weather patterns; the re-emergence of old pestilences and the appearance of new diseases; an increase in UFO activity; serious droughts in several parts of the world, including North America; an increase in severe snowstorms, particularly in the northeastern U.S.; the possible eruption of Mount St. Helens, Mount Rainier or Shasta by the early 1980s (St. Helens actually erupted in May, 1980); an increase in tornadoes and hurricanes and greater earthquake activity—globally as well as in the United States.

The benefit of hindsight enables us to recognize that the predictions noted above have had both general and specific fulfillment in the twenty-plus years since they were first published.

However, the predictions which proved to be accurate are less than half of the prophecies which were given and which should have been fulfilled by the mid-90s, but have not been. And many of the remaining previews of the future are rather bizarre.

Lake says that in the UFO he foresaw unimaginable disasters coming upon North America, triggered by nature's revolt against man's exploitation. His advice: Respect Mother Earth, and if a Native American, return to the sacred dances, rituals and religious ceremonies.

If accepted as factual, the entire episode demonstrates the occult/demonic nature of the UFO encounter which began it all. The significant thing to note is the effect the encounter had upon Lake. By his own admission it left him divorced, sick, unemployed, homeless and destitute. He also became much more open to shamanistic activity and to the old pagan paths, including a form of earth worship.[26]

The UFO effect on people definitely closely parallels the effect of demonic invasion in people's lives.

## Hell at Heaven's Gate

Such was the cover headline on one of the many news magazines which reported on the March 22-24, 1997 mass suicide of thirty-nine "Heaven's

Gate" UFO cultists in Rancho Santa Fe, California.

The tragic event was extensively covered by all the media, partly because of its bizarre nature and partly because of its close connection with the comet Hale-Bopp, which was into its closest approach to earth at the time and was a news item in itself.

The group suicide is an extremely dramatic example of the effect UFO entities can have on people, and an illustration of how deception, believed to be demonic in nature, can be incredibly powerful.

The events that led to the Heaven's Gate mass suicide began in the early 1970s when the cult leader, Marshall Herff Applewhite, was fired from a Houston, Texas college professorship because he was a homosexual. Applewhite, the son of a Presbyterian minister, had attended seminary for a year and held a variety of music-related positions in churches and colleges. The father of two, he was divorced.

Depressed, ashamed, hearing voices and secretive about his homosexuality, he checked into a hospital seeking help. He later told a sister, Louise Winant, that he had had an unspecified "near-death experience" as a result of a heart problem.

While in the hospital he met Bonnie Lu Truesdale Nettles, a nurse, who led him into "a new kind of spirituality." Nettles was an astrologer who had dabbled in numerous metaphysical theologies, combining Christian ritual with paganism, science fic-

tion and millennialism. The two became inseparable, bound by a compulsion to lead people into the
UFO-related spirituality they had discovered.

By 1975 "The Two" as they called themselves
(or "Bo" and "Peep"—because they were "spiritual shepherds") had become "UFO missionaries
extraordinary" as UFO author Brad Steiger called
them in his 1978 book by that title.[27]

Traveling about the western U.S. they re-
cruited followers, particularly in communities
with colleges known for supporting alternative
lifestyles. Waldport, Oregon, where in 1975 there
were great numbers of rootless people into just
such a lifestyle, yielded some twenty new recruits.

The message from "The Two" was that a spaceship would soon arrive to transport believers "to
the next evolutionary level." Joining the cult
meant strict discipline: no sex, no human-level relationships (family contact was completely cut
off), no socializing. The cultists lived communally,
begging for money and food in the early days,
though at the end they were earning an income
through the design of web pages. The internet
also became a method of recruitment.

The theology of the group frequently mutated
over the years. At one point, "The Two" were believed to be the two witnesses of Revelation 11,
who would be killed, but rise again three days
later. After Nettles, who was then called "Ti,"
died of cancer in 1985, the word was that Ti was
the Father and "Do" (Applewhite), the Son. The
core message—that a spaceship was the vehicle

which would take them to heaven's gate—re-mained central, however.

Upon the cult leader's insistence that followers become virtually androgynous, members of the group at the time of their suicide had close-cropped haircuts and identical unisex outfits. Some of the males, including Applewhite, had been castrated.

The mixture of Scripture, science fiction (the cultists were hard-core fans of "Star Trek") and ufology came to a deadly head in early 1997.

## Hale-Bopp Was a Trigger

The huge Hale-Bopp comet, which was spotted on July 22, 1995 by astronomer Alan Hale and amateur stargazer Thomas Bopp, was due to make its nearest approach to earth from mid-March to early April 1997. Already deemed significant by the cultists, their interest increased dramatically when amateur astronomer Chuck Shramek announced in November 1996 that he had photographed "a Saturn-like object" trailing Hale-Bopp.

The cultists' interest reached fever pitch when Courtney Brown, an Emory University professor, subsequently announced that his team of three psychic "remote viewers" had focused on Shramek's object and had determined that it was a spaceship full of aliens. Brown claimed on national radio that he had a photograph taken by a "top-10-university astronomy professor" who said radio signals were coming from the object—showing that it was "intelligently driven."

Though astronomers identified Shramek's object to be a star, Brown's photo was proven to be a hoax and his "professor" a no-show, it didn't matter: The members of Heaven's Gate had their long-awaited signal.

"The marker we've been waiting for . . ." was how they described the supposed spaceship in the "suicide press kits" and internet messages they left behind. Described as gentle people, their suicides were carefully planned, conducted in stages over a three-day period and apparently calmly completed. Thus their "human containers" were voluntarily left behind to enable them to move to the UFO which had arrived to take them to "the next level."

Deception, the great work of demonic beings, is woven throughout this intriguingly bizarre and tragic story, as is a fixation on UFOs, *ET,* "X-Files" and "Star Trek."

There's obviously a connection.[28]

John Weldon in *UFOs: What on Earth Is Happening?*, published in 1976, commented on an earlier UFO cult leader, Allen-Michael Noonan, known as "The Berkley Messiah." Weldon wrote then:

> In the rantings of messiah Allen-Michael Noonan there is a lot of truth. He has hit upon principles of prophecy that are accurate to Scripture, and he has identified Jesus as the true opponent of his heavily occult system. He fits neatly into the Lord's description of false messiahs who mislead many in the latter days. . . .

This is surely Satan's masterpiece—this confusion of science, Scripture, UFOs and the occult. This fearsome combination may very well work![29]

Weldon's comments certainly fit Heaven's Gate and similar groups. There are many of these cults—such as the Raelians, who follow a fifty-one-year-old former race car driver from France in UFO-related beliefs, and adherents of the Unarius Academy of Science, founded over forty years ago by a California couple. The current leader—seventy-six-year-old Charles Spiegal, a retired psychology prof—eagerly awaits 1,000 spaceships from "Myton" around the year 2001 to reclaim the lost continent Atlantis and bring salvation to earth. Followers of the now-deceased channeler Dorothy Martin are awaiting a spaceship commander named Sananda (Jesus) to swoop down in his spaceship and save them, according to messages channeled to Martin.[30]

Certainly this brief and very incomplete overview clearly indicates the devastating effects UFO entities have on those who encounter them or buy into their message. That deceptive effect can be nothing other than the work of demonic beings.

### Reason #4: Their Messages

Already unavoidably alluded to above, the messages purportedly coming from the UFOnauts are an important clue to their nefarious identity. Invariably these messages include *some* biblical truth, but always in a distorted form, and always combined with non-biblical input.

A comment made back in 1968 by the late Walter Martin, founder of the Christian Research Institute, and radio's original "Bible Answer Man," has proven to be prophetic. During an interview I conducted with him, Martin expressed the conviction that UFOs were demonic. He did so long before such a view had gained the wide acceptance it enjoys today.

A member of NICAP and involved in UFO research, Martin said he had personally seen UFOs. He indicated that the dean of a New Jersey seminary with which he was associated as a visiting professor had photographed one in broad daylight as it buzzed the campus.

Martin's comment on the identity of UFOnauts and their messages was insightful. At the time of the interview there had been relatively few CE3 or CE4 encounters, with the notable exception of the Hills incident. Nevertheless, Martin said he believed that at some point in the near future UFO occupants would begin to interact extensively with people.

Their message? "We are superior beings—advanced far beyond you earthlings. Look at our technology. But we have come to help and to guide you. The only condition is that you be willing to forget and go beyond your outmoded religious beliefs and follow our directions."

## He Was Right On

As will be shown, this prediction is incredibly accurate.

Popular New Age author Brad Steiger, who for decades has tracked numerous messages from alleged aliens—often called "Space Brothers"—offers such messages in his book *The Fellowship* as an alternative to traditional Christianity. He writes:

> People of Earth, you are becoming fourth dimensional whether you are ready or not. Leave the old to those who cling to the old. Don't let the New Age pass you by. . . . The Space Beings are doing all they can to help humankind, but they cannot force themselves on us or take control of the conditions here, however bad things might be. . . . Contactees have been told that the Space Beings hope to guide Earth to a period of great unification, when all races will shun discriminatory separations and all humankind will recognize its responsibility to every other life-form existing on the planet. The Space Beings also seek to bring about a single, solidified government, which will conduct itself on spiritual principles and permit all of its citizens to grow constructively in love.[31]

## The Washington Seeress

Ruth Montgomery, for many years a syndicated Washington columnist on politics and world affairs, became internationally known in the 1960s through her book *A Gift of Prophecy* which is the biography of the psychic Jeanne Dixon, who apparently foretold President Kennedy's assassination. Since then Montgomery has devoted her attention to psychic matters and has written a great many books on the subject.

By her own admission she engages in occult activities, having her own "spirit guides" who communicate with her through automatic writing. She was introduced to her guides when famed medium Arthur Ford showed her how to do automatic writing. Daily sessions with the guides have followed for nearly three decades.[32]

And what messages do Ruth Montgomery's guides channel?

> We are all one. Our Space Brothers and Sisters share with us a mutual Creator. . . . The more enlightened among us [earthlings] have had numerous lives on other planets as well as on earth. . . . [A] large group of spacelings have volunteered to . . . become "walk-ins" through the utilization of unwanted human forms.[33]

The guides (who, according to her, insisted she write *Aliens Among Us* about UFOs and extraterrestrials) and who are about to usher in the New Age, told her, "We human souls all began simultaneously as 'sparks from God'—as did the souls in other galaxies. . . . Space beings are now rushing into earth as seldom before to awaken earthlings and help them realize that [unless better ways to settle disputes are found] destruction is imminent."[34]

A space being called Rolf channels, "We are coming in great numbers, not with any intention of harm, but to rescue earth from pollution and nuclear explosions."[35]

And then follows some 200 pages of more of the same, amid fantastic stories about the exploits of "walk-ins," and long messages from "Space Brothers." Among other things, they recommend the use of crystals—for power, healing and success.

The "spirit guides" sign off the book with,

> It is better to lose one's body and preserve one's soul on a higher plateau than to save one's skin by crowding others out of the way and thinking solely of one's own rescue. We are not our soul. We are not our body. That is simply a costume that we are permitted to wear for a brief moment in time, but we, like time, are forever.[36]

Shades of Heaven's Gate!

Montgomery's books, with their potpourri of reincarnation, possession, pantheism and pagan mysticism, are best-sellers, subtly massaging thousands with their message.

## *Communion* to *Breakthrough*

By far the most dramatic and widespread communication of the UFOnaut message has come through the widely successful best-sellers by Whitley Strieber—*Communion, Transformation* and *Breakthrough.*

Strieber, a good writer with moderate success as the author of a number of books in the horror/occult genre, personally had a number of abduction experiences, beginning in December 1985. His book *Communion,*[37] which topped the *New York Times* best-seller list for months on end, was the account of the initial and early experiences. *Transformation,* another best-seller, continued the story of his UFOnaut encounters and began to transmit the messages of the visitors.

Strieber became a UFO celebrity with promotional tours, media interviews, conferences and a *Communion* newsletter. In December 1995, he claimed to have received 139,000 letters, the majority of them from fellow contactees/abductees.

However, in 1990 Strieber appeared to renounce the whole thing, discontinued the newsletter and dropped out of public view. But the jacket copy on his next book, *Breakthrough*, published at the end of his five-year hiatus, tells the real story:

Strieber [during his time out of the public view] has been led by these visitors on an astounding journey of *revelation*, and with their inspiration, has discovered a passageway to profound personal insight. He has seen them enter the lives of others and witnessed the extraordinary effects of their presence. *And he has received their vast wisdom about the wonder of life and the rich, almost totally unexplored experience we call death. . . . Breakthrough gives us a* truly illuminating look at *these mysterious, yet prescient, agents of change and reveals their inspiring message of hope for our chaotic and troubled world* [emphasis mine].[38]

Strieber's proofs (described in *Breakthrough*) of the reality and good intent of his visitors are classic examples of occult/demonic phenomena: rapping (three sets of three knocks),[39] possession, apparitions (including those of dead relatives) and astral travel, to note but a few.[40]

The aliens, through Strieber, present messages like these:

> [L]ive with your sins, taste them, bear them, face what you have done and what you are. That is the direction of freedom. . . .
>
> And then there came into me a tremendous peace, as if every cell in my body had suddenly surrendered. I saw good and evil as one, I saw angels and demons as different aspects of the same vast compassion, and knew that hell is only what we make it, and that mercy is everywhere, in the air, the heart, the old light that sings us through from babyhood. . . .
>
> The darkness had taught me, had drawn me into a new and deeper view, had shown me what the love that is spoken of by Christ and Buddha truly is. . . .

If one could pass beyond guilt, one would come to see sin as integral to the process of resurrection. . . . That was why the residue of evil appeared so beautiful. . . . It is not for nothing that the tree of Eden is called the tree of the knowledge of good and evil. . . .

The veil between the worlds is growing thin. We're on a journey of discovery, not only as individuals, but as an unfolding creation. By emerging, the visitors will disrupt and profoundly change everything and we know it, and that is what all the denial and resistance is about. . . .

I searched through the *Tao te Ching* and the Gospels, to which the visitors had directed me years ago. I found a particular sequence of words taken from both that seemed to offer an exceptional enlargement of meaning: "From before time and space, Tao. It is beyond being. How to see this? Look inside." "In Him was life, and the life was the light of men."[41]

It's a mish-mash of truth and error.

Phil Klass writes insightfully in *UFO Abductions: A Dangerous Game*:

Strieber's remarks suggest that he now sees himself as a modern-day messiah who has been chosen to warn the people of this planet, bringing them not the word of God, but of the omniscient UFOnauts.[42]

It is most interesting to note that the names by which the UFO messengers reveal themselves are frequently the same as those of demonic beings from antiquity. Examples are Ishtar, Chemosh, Moroni, Ashtoreth and so on. In the Apocrophal book of Enoch, chapter 10:4-12, there is a reference to a fallen angel named Semjaza. The similarity of the name to that of the "beautiful blonde female UFOnaut named Semjase from the constellation Pleiades" is striking. The current UFO Semjase has allegedly given messages to Swiss cult leader Billy Meier, UFO author Brad Steiger and numerous other people around the world, foretelling the snatching away of 144,000 people who will be whisked off to the stars![43] It seems quite apparent that more than just the name is the same: the demonizing activity of Semjase or Semjaza is identical.

There can be no question (though we've quoted only a few of the many revealing passages which could be cited from the UFO literature) as to the main thrust of the UFO "revelations." The messages which Strieber and the rest are passing on, purportedly from the aliens, are the very antithesis of the Christian message, though some of that is mixed in too.

The UFO entities are proclaiming reincarnation, a false Jesus and a synthesis of pagan and Christian doctrine that completely negates the truth of salvation alone through the Lord Jesus Christ.

Researchers Nelson Pacheco and Tommy Blann observe that:

Beginning in the early 50s, various UFO contactees such as Adamski and others began to appear, spreading their esoteric messages of "brothers from space" and the beginning of a "New Age" in which these beings would eventually make contact with the Earth. Unknown to the general public at the time, some of these contactees were involved in traditional occult groups and practices such as theosophy, witchcraft and black magic. Others were con artists, some of whom were later arrested on criminal charges.

Many of the UFO cults were (and still are) connected to the shadowy "I AM" group founded by theosophist Guy Ballard in the 1930s. Ballard claimed to have special access to supernatural forces, and channeled various so-called "ascended masters;" among whom were certain Venusians called "The Lords of the Flame." According to this group, Jesus Christ—one of the many Ascended Masters—was a man who developed the "I AM" or "God Self" within himself.[44]

Pacheco and Blann cite researcher David Stupple who says, "If you look at the contactee groups today, you'll see that most of the stable, larger ones are actually neo-I AM groups, with some sort of tie to Ballard's organization."[45]

And running through it all like a thread is the concept which Walter Martin predicted years ago:

The "aliens" are here to guide us with their "superior wisdom and knowledge," and we will be saved if we open up and accept them and their "truth."[46]

The progression in Strieber's view of his visitors as revealed in his three books—from fear, rejection and paranoia over their evil nature, to acceptance, "love" and promotion—is quite remarkable. It gives every appearance of being a growing invasion by the spirit world.

Strieber's statement in *Breakthrough* is significant.

> Contact [with the UFO entities] . . . appears to be intended to direct us toward a power that lies undiscovered within us. . . . As knowledge grows . . . we are beginning to see that something real lies behind the old myths and gods—a strange otherness that is beginning to respond.[47]

Ankerberg and Weldon have summed it up well in their *Facts on UFOs*:

> [W]e have examined scores of such messages [from UFOnauts], and, as many researchers have noted, none can deny that they offer us the same old occultism. Brad Steiger [noted UFO and New Age author], who has investigated hundreds of cases, confesses that "whether men and women claim to be in contact with Space Brothers, As-

cended Masters, or spirits from the astral plane, they are all independently coming up with largely the same communications."[48]

And because of their similarity, I contend that these messages are coming from one source—a demonic one.

Not only do UFO contactees and occult contactees receive similar messages, but they experience similar manifestations and similar offers of spiritual guidance. See Appendix B for an expanded example of this phenomenon.

Messages from the counter-kingdom come in a variety of ways and from a variety of messengers, but their source is the same.

## Reason #5: Their Period of Pervasive Presence

A statistic quoted by Hugh Ross, astronomer, scientist and UFO researcher, caught my attention as I listened to a recording of one of his lectures on UFOs.

Ross stated that he had compiled a chart of the annual number of reported UFO sightings as far back as the 1700s. While admitting that early records tend to be sketchy, his research showed that the number of sightings had "spiked" in 1968 and since then had remained consistently at that high level.[49]

The date caused me to begin reflecting and researching. I recalled that in *Apocalypse Next* (first

published in 1980) I had noted that 1970 seemed
to be something of a watershed, spiritually. As detailed in my book, it was a period in which the occult, particularly witchcraft, seemed to explode
onto the North American scene. Magazines, movies, books—even university courses—were full of
the dark side of the paranormal world.

I recalled hearing Charles Malik, former head of
the U.N., tell a conference audience at Arrowhead
Springs, California in 1979 that a major challenge
then facing the world, including North America,
was the recent global revival of paganism.

Keith Bailey, in his soon-to-be-published book,
*Strange Gods*, describes the amazing rise of animism (belief in, awareness, appeasement, worship
and use of evil spirits) in the Western world in recent years. He writes:

> *Beginning in the 1960s* . . . the debut of hard
> rock music, Woodstock, the general youth
> rebellion and the use of drugs seemed to oc-
> cur simultaneously with widespread de-
> monic manifestations. . . . The religions of
> Native American tribes have revived *over the
> past thirty years* . . . [with] the animists among
> Native Americans actually [being] a small
> minority when compared to the number of
> Caucasians in North America who practice
> animism in one form or another. . . . The in-
> flux of many ethnic groups from all over the
> world has introduced to the United States
> several forms of animism such as voodoo,

**animism** (an′i-mizm), *n.* the theory of
the existence of an immaterial principle
or force, inseparable from matter, to
which all life and action are attributable;
the belief or teaching that the soul is the
vital principle upon which organic development depends.

idolatry, fetishism, fortune-telling and Eastern mysticism. . . . The form of spiritualism
founded in the U.S. by the Fox sisters—purported communication with the dead—is a
movement which claimed as many as 20
million followers in this century [emphasis
mine].[50]

Bailey quotes Dr. Laurence W. Wood, professor of
systematic theology at Asbury Seminary, who wrote
in the Autumn 1996 issue of *The Asbury Herald*:

In popular television programs and movies for families, you see grotesque demonic
creatures who symbolize our aggressiveness
and anxious fears. The postmodern world is
a world of hobgoblins, fairies, divination and
superstition. One might think that these are
not taken seriously in real life, but the recent
rapid growth of the New Age Movement indicates otherwise.

Dr. Bailey comments:

Dr. Wood rightly draws attention to the
[recent] resurgence of interest in demons in
the arts. Not only is it evident in television
and Hollywood, but in a whole new genre of
modern novels devoted to horror. This level
of preoccupation with the world of evil spirits has not been around since the Middle
Ages. . . . It would appear that our sophisti-

cated, high-tech, intellectual Western civilization may produce the lowest and darkest forms of demonic worship in all of human history. Those of us who take seriously the prophetic Scriptures should not be surprised at this turn of events . . . as animism permeates the culture and seriously competes for the souls of men. The [current] level of demonic activity in the West can only be compared to the first century.[51]

I remembered reading in John Weldon's *UFOs: What on Earth Is Happening?*:

Poltergeists [spirits] have long been connected with UFO flaps. John Keel [well-known author and UFO researcher] plotted a graph of poltergeist reports and UFO flaps . . . and found them highly coordinated. Poltergeist flaps seem to precede, closely follow, or occur simultaneously with UFO flaps.[52]

And as I reflected, from a paradigm that UFOs are demonic, that UFO sightings and encounters had peaked in 1968, I became more convinced than ever that the period was indeed a watershed. With this exception: By pinpointing a single year in *Apocalypse Next* I was undoubtedly focusing too narrowly. It was more like several years—from the mid-60s to the mid-70s.

Consider the events of that brief period of history in terms of it being a spiritual watershed:

- 1963—Prayer and Bible reading declared unconstitutional in U.S. schools.
- 1960 to early 1970s—A youth counter-culture flourished, characterized by antigovernment and antiauthority attitudes, anti-Vietnam riots and demonstrations, Woodstock-style hedonism, widespread drug use and similar expressions of rebellion and rejection of traditional standards, typified by the hippie movement.
- 1960 and onward—The sexual "revolution," as the media termed it, created a new morality. *Newsweek* magazine documented the sweeping changes in their November 13, 1967 issue: "The old taboos are dying. A new, more permissive society is taking shape. . . . And, behind this expanding permissiveness is . . . a society that has lost its consensus on such crucial issues as premarital sex . . . marriage, birth control and sex education."[53]
- Mid-1960s—A massive invasion of North America by Eastern religions, New Age teachings and spiritism began. This is especially significant because at least one previous attempt to "mainstream" these philosophies had failed.[54]
- 1960 and onward—Homosexuals began "coming out of the closet" in increasing numbers and started pushing for acceptance in militant fashion. Yet it was only in 1979 that the American Psychiatric Association removed homosexuality from its list of mental disorders.
- 1970—The World Council of Churches de-

cided that the word "church" in their name should no longer be confined to Christian but should encompass people of all faiths, or no faith. Their decision tied in well with their policy of funding Marxist rebels in various countries.[55]

* 1973—Abortion was legalized.

Certainly it is possible to read too much into the traumatic events of the era we've just considered. But anyone with spiritual perception would have to agree that it was a watershed time. Even the media now refers back to the period prior to those years as being a different time—an era of innocence, as characterized by TV shows such as "Leave It to Beaver."

The late Francis Schaeffer, generally acknowledged to be the foremost evangelical philosopher/theologian of the late twentieth century, wrote the following in his 1979 volume *Whatever Happened to the Human Race?*:

> [T]he consensus of our society no longer rests on a Judeo-Christian base but rather on a humanistic one. . . . *In our time humanism has replaced Christianity* as the consensus of the West [emphasis mine].[56]

And without doubt a strong UFO upsurge in that time, and increasingly since, was and is a factor in the recent dramatic growth of the occult and New Age spirituality. Even New Age author and prolific UFO writer Brad Steiger has noticed the connection.[57]

Keith Bailey in *Strange Gods* makes an interesting point:

> All the major redemptive events in biblical history have been accompanied by a resurgence of demonic manifestation. Since Satan was once an angel he has extensive knowledge of spiritual things and always seeks to withstand spiritual breakthroughs in the unfolding of God's plans. According to the book of Revelation the demon hordes will be let loose on the earth in unprecedented numbers during the dark days of the Great Tribulation. It seems that demon activity even now is being stepped up in anticipation of end-time events.[58]

## Conclusion

On the basis of the evidence offered here, I am convinced that the UFOnauts are unquestionably demonic, a conclusion with which even agnostics such as Harvard psychiatrist John Mack and astrophysicist/UFO researcher Jacques Vallee agree. Mack writes:

> [UFO entities and the] UFO abductions experience . . . bear resemblance to other dramatic, transformative experiences undergone by shamans, mystics, and ordinary citi-

zens who have had encounters with the paranormal. . . . The aliens appear to be consummate shape-shifters. . . . This shamanistic dimension needs further study. These phenomena cannot be understood within the framework of the laws of Western science.[59]

And Vallee says,

The same power attributed to saucer entities was once the exclusive property of fairies, witches, shamans and the like.[60]

Politically correct or not, the facts crowd us to only one conclusion: the UFOnauts are demonizing entities!

# CHAPTER NINE

## *Entry Points for Demonization*

An interesting and instructive fact has drawn my attention as I have researched the UFO/demonization connection.

It is the fact that most, if not all, of the recorded cases of abductions are of people who have had some previous occult involvement.

Hugh Ross, in a recorded lecture, claimed that people with "open doors" to the occult see UFOs at an incredibly higher rate than those without. He goes so far as to state, based on his research, that there is—almost without exception—a one-for-one correspondence of UFO CE4 and CE5 encounters and prior occult activity.

Certainly, the cases I have studied show a similar major connection.

For example, all the abductees profiled in John Mack's *Abduction*, with one possible exception, had occult involvement of one kind or another prior to their UFO experiences. Their prior occult connections included talking with spirits, intense interest in Eastern religions and the paranormal, experimentation with mind-altering drugs, family involvement in Tibetan Buddhism, the practice of yoga and meditation, out-of-body experiences, a family history of psychic activity, sexual immorality and an expressed desire to be "taken" by extraterrestrials.[1]

Famous UFO abductee and author Whitley Strieber has an extensive background in the occult. By his own account he has been involved in Zen Buddhism, tarot cards, witchcraft, altered states of consciousness, alchemy, Tibetan charting, meditation and a study of the teachings of the occult mystics Gurdjieff and Ouspenjsky. Prior to the release of *Communion* he was a writer of fiction in the horror/occult genre. In the foreword to the 1989 re-release of *Catmagic*, described as "a tale of modern witchcraft," Strieber writes:

> I wrote *Catmagic* in 1984, well before I was consciously aware of the visitors who figure in *Communion*.
>
> *Communion* is the story of how it felt to have personal contact with the visitors. The mysterious small beings that figure prominently in *Catmagic* seem to be an unconscious rendering of [the visitors], created before I was aware that they may be real.[2]

William Alnor quotes Strieber as saying, in an interview with the author of *Faces of Fear*:

I am a student of the great thirteenth-century mystic Meister Eckhart. I have been a witch. I have experimented with the worship of earth as a goddess/mother.[3]

Yet another confirmation comes in Dr. Karla Turner's *Into the Fringe*. This intriguing book details the deeply disturbing story of the devastation and disruption effected in the life of her family as a result of numerous UFO abductions. Occult involvement by family members preceded the encounters.[4]

The same is true of the case studies from the Conference on ET Abductions held at MIT in 1992, as reported in C.B.D. Bryan's book. Each abductee whose story is recounted had prior occult involvement.[5]

*The Mysterious Valley*, Christopher O'Brien's book on the numerous ongoing UFO and paranormal events in the rugged San Luis Valley, indicates the same.[6] And in *Encounters: Case Studies of Extraterrestrial Abductions*, by psychiatrist Dr. Edith Fiore, the pattern holds true—though some of the hypnotic regressions detailed in this book seem extremely farfetched.[7]

## What Should Be Avoided?

If occult involvement invites demonic invasion, or at least makes it far more likely, it makes great sense to avoid, as one would avoid the plague, such involvement. What sort of activities should be avoided?

Or to put it another way, what are the pas-
sageways which spirits from the dark world util-
ize to move into human lives? What kind of
activities and practices create doorways for demonization?

As a preface to a specific answer, consider these
basic truths: Sin, which is the breaking of the
moral law of God, leads to spiritual bondage and
death (Romans 6:23). The Bible says that *all* have
sinned and come short of the standard (or glory)
of God (3:23). And sin carries with it the penalty
of eternal death, decreed by the holiness and justice of God. However, because of God's love, it is
gloriously possible to be forgiven, set free and
given the gift of eternal life. It happens through
confession of sin, repentance and faith in what the
Lord Jesus Christ did when He paid the penalty
for sin by His death upon the cross. I will speak
more on this vital topic later.

While every sin is destructive to a degree, there
are certain sinful activities and actions which, because of their nature and focus on the demonic,
become open doorways for invasion by the dark
spirit world.

A catalog of such thresholds includes, but is not
limited to, the following:

### Mind-altering drugs

In Revelation 9:21 the Apostle John writes of a
group of people whom he foresees as experiencing
the awesome judgments of God. However, rather
than changing their ways, they are described as

not repenting "of their murders, their magic arts, their sexual immorality or their thefts" (NIV).

The word translated "magic arts" ("sorceries" in some versions) is very significant. It comes from the Greek *pharmakeia* which is the word from which we get our English "pharmacy," or drugstore. It means a drug-related kind of occult worship or black magic.

There can be little question that Satan uses hallucinogenic drugs to take people to deep levels of influence and control through demonization. The individual mentioned in chapter 7, whom I, along with others, had the privilege of helping to find deliverance from deep entanglement in witchcraft and demonic control, confirms from personal experience and observation that this is so.

McCandlish Phillips has identified "a direct and mysterious relationship between certain chemical agents and the supernatural. Certain drugs can carry the user into the realm of the demonic." He writes:

> By taking these agents into his or her body, a person opens up avenues into his or her soul and spirit by which evil spirits may enter and seize a measure of control. . . . I call them chemical-supernatural agents because these drugs can, and frequently do, introduce people to the supernatural. . . . [They] provide a shortcut to the supernatural.[8]

:areful research, this award-winning jour-
documented the fact that drugs like pey-
), marijuana, alcohol, narcotics, "sacred
mushrooms" and hallucinogens really do open up
avenues of contact with unseen evil spirits.

### *Illicit sexual activity*

Based on his extensive research into the subject,
McCandlish Phillips has also written:

> Satan loves to corrupt people sexually. He
> will do it wholesale if possible. Sexual sins of
> the grossest kinds are spawned and pro-
> moted by Satan in direct association with
> occult practices.[9]

The literature dealing with demonization is full
of case studies of individuals who have become involved through illicit sexual behavior. As Foster
observes, not every improper sexual act results in
demonization, but it is unquestionably an avenue
consistently utilized by the enemy to move into
human lives. This is so, quite apparently, because
sexual experiences have the ability, as someone
has written, "to penetrate to the very depths of the
personality."

The Bible makes it clear, in the words of Jesus,
that God designed marriage to be the union of one
man and one woman who would, in sexual inter-
course, become "one flesh" (Matthew 19:1-6). The
Apostle Paul warned against sexual involvement
with a prostitute, declaring that the one who does

so becomes "one flesh" with her (1 Corinthians 6:16). The writer of Proverbs revealed the truth that the person who commits adultery "destroyeth his own soul"—his capacity to reason, feel or decide properly (Proverbs 6:32).

This most intimate of all human relationships is even used in biblical imagery (husband/wife, bridegroom/bride) as an illustration of the relationship between God and His people. Because sexual union is so significant, it is no wonder that it is the object of the enemy's attack.

Satan hates whatever God has created or designed. Consequently, since God designed marriage to be the setting within which pure, wholesome sexual relationships are to occur, it is no surprise to learn that sex outside the wise boundaries which the Creator has established should be an avenue for demonization.

The sexual sins of fornication, adultery, voluntary incest, homosexuality, bestiality, prostitution and solicitation of prostitutes are all potential doors of entry for demonic spirits. Pornography, whether visual (magazines, films, videos, TV or internet) or verbal (phone sex), can also open the door to invasion.

Even secular journalists have discerned the sexual/occult connection. A special occult-themed issue of *Mademoiselle*, the cover of which promised "Sorcery and Sex," included an interview with Harry E. Wedeck, a college professor with an extensive knowledge of the history of witchcraft. The interviewer commented, "Whenever I've read about the occult there've always *seemed to* be strong links between sorcery and sex—and very sick sex at that." Wedeck replied, "Witchcraft often attracted people of unbridled or frustrated sexual desires. And even if you were possessed of neither, you couldn't be a witch unless you gave yourself completely to it. . . ."[10]

Reseachers who have recorded case studies of demonization have indicated that such illicit sexual activity can be, and frequently is, an invitation—usually unintentional—to evil spirits to enter one's life.[11] It's a major threshold.

### Satanic music

Over twenty-five years ago Phillips, with keen insight and prophetic vision, wrote:

> There is something more to rock 'n roll than just music throbbing in the air. Some of it has spiritual dynamism, and some of it is a throwback to tribal ritual. You can "groove" on it. Go into any of the dark areas of the world where demonic religions hold sway, and you will find tribes whose members at times dance themselves into frenzy to the vibration of loud, drumming music. Such music sometimes has an evil energy that produces violence.
>
> This is not a blanket condemnation of the rock idiom; it is not all of a piece. However, it should be recognized that there are spiritual effects attending the use of some of it.

Let me quote a paragraph from a story about the religious use of rock music that ran in the *Times*:

"The music lets your consciousness expand," said Joe Frazier, a student at the Berkeley Divinity School in New Haven whose group, the Eschaton, performed at the Yale service. "It brings out a sense of community and some fantastic commerce with the spirit and the soul."

That is exactly so. Evil powers produce such effects in the human soul and spirit through the impulses and vibrations of such music, and some of this music involves a commerce with evil spirits. That is why rock concerts of the more frenzied kind have sometimes been immediately followed by outbreaks of violence. Spiritually, that kind of rock music is an emergence of tribalism in North America.[12]

The kind of music about which Phillips wrote in 1970 was tame compared to what is happening today. Increasingly over the years, many rock musicians have, both in their music and their proclamations, shown themselves to be openly satanic. In numerous instances, their lyrics leave little doubt about it and their lifestyles demonstrate it.

An example is the Marilyn Manson band. Named for its leader, the members of the band have each taken the name of a deceased celebrity as a first name and the name of a mass killer as a

second name. Manson himself is unabashedly devoted to the satanic, both in his public perfor-
mances (which often entail blasphemous parodies
of Christianity) and in his personal life. As one fan
put it, "He doesn't just perform it—he lives it," referring to Manson's satanism. Manson was selling
as many as 20,000 CDs a week in early 1997,
spreading a blatantly satanic message.[13]

Danzig, the German satanist band recently ac-
quired by the Disney Corporation, is another
tragic example. Openly utilizing "in-your-face"
unvarnished satanic lyrics and props, the group
styles itself as the epitome of evil.[14]

MTV, the rock music network, is rife with the
kind of music, and far worse, about which Phillips
wrote. It has a tremendous impact on the youth of
North America. When the billions of dollars spent
on such music in CDs, cassettes, videos and concerts is factored in, the effect is almost incalculable. Particularly when it is noted that Andrew
Fletcher of Saltoun, writing centuries ago about
the powerful effect of music in a culture, said, "If
a man were permitted to write the ballads, he
need not care who should make the laws of a nation."

Music, unquestionably, is a major potential entry path for demonization.

### Satanic games and toys

A veritable avalanche of such toys and games
has descended upon the shelves of stores today.

There are the old standbys: ouija boards, tarot

cards, Dungeons and Dragons® and the like. There can be little question that such games have a well-documented history of evil effect on those who indulge in them—even on those who do so somewhat "innocently."

Added to these recently are the myriad of video games, a high percentage of which have occult and even demonic overtones. The addictive nature of these games is certainly a warning flag.

Also of fairly recent vintage are the numerous truly bizarre figures and toys, ranging from the u-biquitous trolls to incredibly grotesque, completely unnatural creations which appear to be a deliberate attack upon normality. Since God is the author of order and decency in creation, the creation of the wildly bizarre thus affects, subtly, the concept of the normative creative order and indirectly of the Creator.

Games and toys such as the above, if not actual doorways to the occult in an individual, can have the effect of conditioning their users for demonization.

### Seances and astrology

Considered by some to be in the category of a parlor game, seances are definitely potential doorways to demonization. This kind of activity is a deliberate, open invitation to spirit beings to manifest themselves, and the demons are happy to oblige.

Another popular activity, dangerous but deemed harmless, is astrology, with its practical application of the use of horoscopes as a means of personal guidance.

As indicated in the article "Star-Struck" in the July 1997 issue of *LIFE* magazine,

> Astrology is hotter than it's been in four centuries. . . . According to a recent poll 48 percent of Americans say astrology is probably or definitely valid. . . . Horoscopes run in a vast majority of dailies. . . . Twenty years ago there were an estimated 1,000 professional astrologers in the United States; today there are something like 5,000. In 1968 . . . the annual market for astrology books was around five million. Today it is closer to twenty million. Netniks can surf thousands of Web sites, devoted to . . . horoscopes.[15]

The author of the *LIFE* article frankly acknowledges that astrology's roots are in the ancient pagan Babylonian culture. His use of terms like "occult," "soothsayers" and "yogi"; his "conversation with 'masters' such as Krishnamurti and the Dalai Lama"; and his approving references to the psychic Jillian and the Vedic (Hindu) astrologer Chakrapaui Ullal all indicate the nature of this pseudo-scientific religion.

And in many other parts of the world, such as Brazil, Europe and Asia, the fascination with astrology is even greater than it is in the U.S. It is very popular and is generally taken seriously.

But it is dangerous.

Isaiah 47:10-15 includes astrology in a list of occult practices which God condemns and against which He warns Israel. Astrology is thus unquestionably a potential doorway to demonization. The fact that it has virtually exploded in popularity since the mid-1960s is most significant.

### Literature

An incredible flood of books, magazines and comics with an occult slant has poured out of the publishing houses of America in recent years.

*Publishers' Weekly* consistently contains advertisements and announcements of new occult releases and New Age publications. A recent issue was devoted to the theme of the paranormal, witchcraft, astrology and the New Age. A somewhat typical ad offered "A Witch's Calendar. Pagan holidays, spells, lore, recipes and more for the compleat witch."[16] Most secular bookstores have large sections of occult books, while some stores are completely devoted to such material. Science fiction, fantasy, horror and erotica frequently have occult aspects. Children are targeted by bizarre comics and by books like the popular *Goosebumps* series of horror best-sellers.

At one point in 1996, prolific author Stephen King's horror fiction occupied five slots on the *New York Times* best-seller list. In *Desperation*, King's early 1997 novel, a demon named Tak, trapped in an abandoned mine for centuries, is set free and takes possession of a man who lives nearby. The demon's problem is that its superhuman energy quickly wears out the body of its human host, and Tak must find a new host. So Tak kills humans whom it can't use and feeds on the psychic energy thus released.

People pay nearly thirty dollars to immerse themselves in this hideous fantasy. Why? Perhaps because King's stories show that evil exists but can be defeated by human effort. Also, perhaps because in *Desperation* evil is random and demonic in nature, meaning that humans have no responsibility. The serial killer murders because he is demon possessed. It's not his fault; he had no choice in the matter. God is powerless to deal with this evil and can only hope His human creations can overcome it by their own wiles.[17]

It is not difficult to see how fiction of this type can open thresholds to demonization.

Another category of books increasingly available to the North American reader is that of the "sacred scriptures" of Eastern religions, such as *The Tibetan Book of the Dead, The Bhagavad-Gita, Three Ways of Asian Wisdom and Hinduism* and so on.

Since the human mind is, in large measure, programmed by what is put into it, the widespread availability of reading material such as the above is bound to have an effect. And the mind filled with occultic or demonic input will invariably affect the will (the control center of one's being), making possible more spirit invasion.

### Movies, TV, videos and the internet

*Rosemarie's Baby*, *The Amityville Horror* and *The Exorcist* were some of the early movies produced by major studios that focused on demonization and the paranormal. Since their release in the late '60s and early '70s, they have proven to be the forerunners of a flood of movies, TV programs and videos which present the occult, the spirit world and the New Age—often in a favorable light.

In addition, an increasing number of films in the horror genre, such as the "Friday the Thirteenth" series, as well as those with openly satanic themes, have massaged the collective North American mind.

Messages conveyed via the motion picture medium have tremendous power to impact. When those messages focus on the occult, the bizarre, the sexual, the violent and the satanic, they powerfully condition the mind and open up wide avenues by which demonization is accomplished.

According to Douglas Groothuis, in "Technoshamanism: Digital Deities in Cyberspace,"

[T]he almost unlimited horizons of cyberspace have become a compelling milieu for those seeking spiritual meaning. Ease of communication, mind-boggling arrays of images, and the ability to interact with others in a fantasy world make cyberspace a popular destination for New Age seekers. . . .

[T]he late Timothy Leary . . . father of LSD, was as convinced of the consciousness-altering possibilities of cyberspace as he had been of psychedelic drugs. Cyberspace, suggests Gen-X guru Douglas Rushkoff and friend of Leary, enables an experience similar to psychedelic drugs. . . .

Pursuing such experiences in cyberspace has been dubbed technoshamanism. In tribal cultures, the shaman played a significant role in village life by serving as a mediator between the community he represented and the spiritual realm. His experiences, often mystical and ecstatic, laid the foundation for his bringing others in the village into contact with the transcendent spiritual reality he'd experienced. Cyberspace offers the promise of similar experiences without the mediating role of the shaman. Cyberspace is becoming a new sacred realm of exploration and enlightenment. . . .

Technoshamanism uses new technologies in the age-old search for meaning and power apart from God's revelation of objective truth.[18]

Such a search has great potential to open a door to demonization.

### *Satanic artifacts*

Fetishes—objects which have been dedicated to demons and which are somehow inhabited by them—are a normal aspect of life in many areas of the world. One of the first actions of new Christians in other lands is often the burning of their fetishes as an act of severing all ties with the demonic.

Not too surprisingly, objects with occult and/or satanic connections are becoming more evident throughout North America. These may be items picked up in other lands as curios but which have been part of demonic ritual, or New Age paraphernalia such as crystals, idols, talismans, charms, good luck objects and so on.

Ed Murphy is recognized as one of the world's foremost authorities in the matter of spiritual warfare. In his massive volume *The Handbook for Spiritual Warfare* he describes an experience which he and his wife had with their oldest daughter when she was a teenager, at a time before he had become knowledgeable about the spirit world.

His daughter Carolyn was a Christian, and normally a sweet-tempered, well-adjusted girl. Then, while he was away at a conference his wife called, asking him to return home at once because she was convinced that their daughter was demonized.

Murphy arrived late, after Carolyn was in bed. Awakening her, he explained to her what his wife had told him.

Within moments her usually sweet personality changed into something evil. With a strange glare in her eyes, she screamed at him, "Leave me alone!"

After Murphy forbade the demons, in Jesus'

name, to speak through Carolyn, she calmed down. Prayer followed, but she had difficulty praying. It was then that Murphy noticed a small object that looked like a Star of David on a chain around Carolyn's neck, to which he had paid little attention previously.

He learned it had been given to her by her boyfriend. It turned out to be, not a Star of David, but a pentagram, a symbol of the occult world.

It was removed, Carolyn confessed and renounced her occult involvement, her recent interest in heavy metal rock music and her rebellious attitude and selfishness. After a brief struggle it appeared that the evil spirits had gone.

But at 2 a.m. Carolyn banged on her parents' bedroom door, crying that the demons were after her again—they seemed to be coming from under her bed, trying to get control of her.

Murphy asked his daughter what she had under her bed. She said, "I have a small box filled with more of those stars and other paraphernalia. I forgot about them when we were praying. Dad, please get them out from under my bed."

Murphy wisely insisted that Carolyn had to do so herself as well as personally destroy them out in the backyard. He accompanied her as she did so, thus making a declaration to the spirit world that she was, by her own will, making a break with them.

Confession and the renouncing of transcendental meditation and the heavy rock music to which her friend had introduced her, as well as the destruction of the offensive music and all other items in her possession which had any connection to the occult, brought genuine spiritual freedom.

That experience and the lessons learned through it launched Ed Murphy into a global ministry of alerting the Church to the reality of the demonic threat.[19]

From personal experience with the individual described in chapter 7, I know that artifacts such as these can be avenues of access which are utilized by the counter-kingdom. I also recall the unusual fashion in which such an artifact burned, including the emitting of strange noises, when we destroyed it by fire. I can't fully explain it, but I've seen it.

### Overt satanism, witchcraft or New Age/Eastern religions

It should be apparent that any of the above, regardless of the religious terminology used, are doorways to the demonic. In this connection the comments of researcher McCandlish Phillips are most instructive:

> Canada and the United States are filling up with . . . new gods . . . coming in from the East as fast as Satan can import them. . . . The satanic forces of darkness are not deployed uniformly among the nations, and demonic activity is by no means equal in all areas of the world. Some nations are under far heavier demonic occupation than others, and in those areas the activity of evil spirits

is far more pronounced. There are places in which Satan and his demons have had great influence, precisely because of the extent of idolatry, false religion and occultism in those places. . . . The rising indulgence in idolatry, false Eastern religions, occultism, spiritualism and immorality gives Satan the occasion he needs to loose more and more demons upon our population.[20]

Any involvement with witchcraft (whether it is called "white" or not), Satanism or Eastern religions (in which demonization invariably plays a role) opens one to the possibility of demonic attack or demonization.

### Rebellion

The prophet Samuel, centuries ago, enunciated an eternal principle which is enshrined in the Scriptures. He said, "Rebellion is as the sin of witchcraft" (1 Samuel 15:23).

A rebellious spirit, which rejects and opposes all authority, is a dangerous one. It undoubtedly is a reflection of the spirit of Satan himself, who chose to rebel against God and who drew with him a third of the angels—spirits which became the dark forces that have troubled mankind since the dawn of human history.

While authority is often wrong, given mankind's fallen nature, to rebel is not the way to right wrongs. It can, in fact, invite the invasion of the cruelest master of all.

## Counterfeit religious experiences

Dr. K. Neill Foster in *Discernment, the Powers and Spirit-Speaking*, while not at all denying the existence of a valid gift of tongues, marshals convincing evidence, as briefly described in chapter 8, for the existence of counterfeit spirit-speaking (tongues), through which people are demonized. Over a dozen recognized ministers, authors, college or seminary professors and Christian leaders who have had extensive experience in the exorcism of evil spirits are cited by Foster. These authorities agree that a high percentage of spirit-speakers (those who speak in an unknown tongue or so-called "heavenly language") have been deceived and demonized. There is danger in opening one's spirit to unknown powers—even if the assumption is that it is the power of God which is sought.[21]

Foster quotes Ferguson, who asserts that

> Repetitive, rhythmic sensory stimuli—whether dancing, flickering lights . . . pounding drums or reiterated syllables—effectively synchronize brain-wave activity and produce altered states of consciousness . . . an excited state, favorable to spirit working.[22]

Spiritualist mediums all over the world often speak in foreign languages when in a trance. The famous medium Mirabelli of Brazil, in trance, spoke twenty-five languages which ordinarily were unknown to him.[23]

Along with the drive to have the tongues experience and its purported spiritual power—most prevalent in charismatic circles—there are a great many strange religious groups on the current scene, particularly in North America. The *U.S. News and World Report* article "The eternal quest for a new age" explored this fact:

Marshall Applewhite's Heaven's Gate cult exemplified the current fascination with paranormal phenomena, self-exploration, and spirituality. The United States has some 3,500 "new" religious groups today, some with beliefs as bizarre as Applewhite's. The New Age has a number of spiritual meccas, among them San Francisco and Santa Cruz, California; Eugene, Oregon; Boulder, Colorado; Santa Fe, New Mexico; Sedona, Arizona and Madison, Wisconsin.

Gnosticism, put down as a heresy by the early Christian church, has resurfaced in the New Age movement. Its primary belief is that self-knowledge is knowledge of God, and that the self and God are one.

According to *Forbes* magazine, Americans spend nearly $2 billion on aromatherapists, channelers, macrobiotic foods, and other New Age items. A 1994 Roper poll showed that of those who practice meditation 45% said it gave them "a strong sense of being in the presence of something sacred."[24]

That same week *TIME* considered "The lure of the cult" and observed:

> Out of the dissatisfaction of the '60s came the spiritual-seekers of the '70s. Cultic groups . . . were formed out of rebellious rubble, culminating in the death of 900 people in Jonestown and 39 in California.[25]

As amply documented through numerous tragic events like Jonestown and Heaven's Gate, false, pseudo-Christian religious pursuits can be thresholds for demonization.

### But what of other events?

A logical question arises at this point. If, in fact, UFOs are demonizing entities which primarily encounter people who have had prior occult involvement, how does one explain Arnold's experience, Roswell, Mantell's UFO-related death and so on? What about the UFO sightings of my five friends who were either theological students or Christian ministers?

There are several possible explanations. First, as we've already noted, these events may be among those that can be explained in terms of natural causes or hoaxes. Second, I still contend that at least some of the events were real experiences—and demonic. The principle of susceptibility is not ruled out simply because we do not know, specifically, what was the prior occult involvement of those who saw or encountered UFOs. Occult involvement, even extensive, may have been present.

Third, in the case of the Christians who sighted UFOs, it is important to note that the Bible and history both indicate that Christians frequently encounter the dark world. Even the Lord Jesus Christ confronted the demonic realm on numerous occasions during His earthly ministry.

The key word we have chosen to use is *primarily*: UFO encounters come *primarily*, though not exclusively, to those with prior occult involvement. However, in the case of abductees, it appears that it may be exclusively so.

Such UFO encounters appear to be suited to the age in which they occur. Consequently our technological space age should expect to have the kind of technological/extraterrestrial manifestations which we're actually seeing!

Thresholds. Points of entry. Avenues on which the dark spirits of the unseen world can stride into a life. They've multiplied in our culture, even as UFO encounters and experiences have dramatically increased.

The correlation is no accident.

# CHAPTER TEN

# *The Profile of Demonization in Scripture*

Does the Bible have anything to say about UFOs? Not specifically.

However, many people believe that it does describe them by inference. The theories range from the ridiculous to the barely plausible, as there have been numerous attempts to find UFOs in the pages of Scripture.

*The Bible and Flying Saucers* by liberal theologian Barry Downing—a 1968 book which has gone through a number of printings, the latest in 1989—is typical of efforts to relate the Bible to what some believe about UFOs.

Downing's view is that the miraculous events of Scripture were actually accomplished by UFOs. According to him, the pillar of cloud by day and fire by night, which the Book of Exodus says led the children of Israel from Egypt to Canaan, was a

UFO; it was a UFO that parted the Red Sea and Moses encountered a UFO at the burning bush and on Mount Sinai when he received the Ten Commandments.

Biblical angels, even the godly variety, were actually extraterrestrials, says Downing. The vision which the prophet Ezekiel had of the "wheel in a wheel" was a sighting of a UFO. Elijah's chariot of fire, the star of Bethlehem, Christ's transfiguration and ascension, the light that blinded the Apostle Paul and led to his conversion—all these and more were related to UFO activity.[1] The net effect of this approach is to remove the supernatural from Scripture.

Others take the highly offensive position that a UFOnaut visited the Virgin Mary and artificially impregnated her![2]

John Weldon's comment on such teaching is noteworthy. He says,

> Saucer theologians . . . are invariably weak on scholarship. This includes even the "scholarly" attempts (e.g., Joseph Blumrich's *The Spaceships of Ezekiel*). They are inconsistent, violate accepted methods of interpretation, ignore contextual considerations, disregard cultural and historical matters, delete or amend the text to support their views, believe the Bible is unreliable or mythological, etc. In reviewing fifteen of these books, Dr. Robert S. Elwood of the University of Southern California concludes

they are a "hopeless mass of woolly theories and garbled facts" by authors who were obviously ignorant of the language and cultures of ancient books.[3]

The late Dr. Walter Martin, founder of Christian Research Institute, in a 1987 taped message, said:

> First, does the Bible talk about UFOs at all? Theologically, categorically, flat out, no! You can try and read a UFO into Ezekiel's wheel within a wheel [but] wheels within wheels with eyes running around them are not necessarily portals on revolving saucers. The Bible doesn't mention UFOs by name.[4]

Most biblical scholars see Ezekiel's description of "a wheel in the middle of a wheel" (Ezekiel 1:16) as not an early UFO sighting but a vision of heaven and the throne of God, which God gave to the prophet. A parallel vision given to the Apostle John is recorded in the fourth chapter of Revelation. I would therefore agree with Martin: The Bible doesn't mention UFOs by name.

But the Bible *does* have a great deal to say about Satan, the counter-kingdom and the diabolical legions that comprise and promote his evil spiritual empire. Weldon writes with keen insight:

> Since Scripture says that in the last times Satan will come upon the world with "all

power and signs and false wonders, and with all deception of wickedness" and that God will allow "wonders in the sky above," a phenomenon like Satanic UFOs could almost be expected as our age draws to a close.

Ephesians 2:2 refers to Satan when it speaks of "the prince of the *power* of the *air.*" In the original Greek, the word "power" (*exousia*) is a collective term meaning the whole empire of evil spirits, and the "air" (*aer*) means physical air in the normal sense. The center of Satan's power, according to this verse, is the atmosphere around the earth. If the air is the region of the demons' might, we can easily see the UFO interconnection that could exist. All in all, everything one would expect in spiritual warfare and deception can be found in the UFO phenomena.[5]

Inasmuch as we believe and have shown that UFOnauts are, in fact, expressions of supernatural evil, it follows that the Word of God has much to say about UFOs—not specifically, but by clear inference.

And just what does the Bible say?

It says that the dark angels are part of an organized army—with ranked groupings under the ultimate command of Satan, the chief of the fallen spirits. The Bible makes it clear that these foul spirits are the deadly adversaries of mankind; that they seek to be worshiped and that they can and do possess people. In fact, possession appears to be what they deeply desire: to be in control of a body—preferably human, but failing that, animal.

Evil spirits can prophesy, though not with complete accuracy, and often (because their commander is a liar and the "father of lies") they are deliberately misleading. Most significantly, in the light of our investigation, the counter-kingdom is predicted in Scripture to become increasingly active in the closing days of human history.

## Check It Out

Let's look at the actual words of Scripture that bear out what we have summarized above concerning the Bible's teaching on demonization. But first a word about the Bible, which is far and away the world's all-time best-seller.

The Bible claims to be the inspired, infallible Word of God and, in spite of many vicious attacks upon it over the centuries, it gives every evidence to the intellectually honest seeker of being just what it claims to be. To present the evidence for the authenticity and authorship of the Bible is beyond the scope of this book. Besides, it has already been done by many scholars far more able than this writer. I particularly recommend Josh McDowell's excellent *Evidence That Demands a Verdict* and *More Evidence That Demands a Verdict*, as well as *The Signature of God*, an outstanding volume by Grant Jeffery.

## What the Bible Says about Demons

*Demons are ranked in what is called
"principalities and powers"*

Like an army, the dark angels are arrayed in ranks, being described as "principalities and powers," under the control and command of Satan, who is called "the chief of the fallen spirits."

> *Daniel 10:12-13:* Then he [a mighty angelic being] said unto me, Fear not, Daniel: for from the first day that thou didst set thine heart to understand, and to chasten thyself before thy God, thy words were heard, and I am come for thy words. But the *prince of the kingdom of Persia* [understood to be the most powerful demon assigned to that nation] withstood me one and twenty days: but, lo, Michael, one of the chief princes [an archangel], came to help me. (italics mine)

> *John 16:11:* [Jesus said] . . . *the prince of this world* [a term applied to Satan] is judged. (italics mine)

> *Ephesians 2:2:* Wherein in time past ye walked according to the course of this world, according to *the prince of the power of the air*, the spirit that now worketh in the children of disobedience. (italics mine)

*Ephesians 3:10:* To the intent that now unto *the principalities and powers* in heavenly places might be known by the church the manifold wisdom of God. (italics mine)

*Ephesians 6:10-13:* Finally, my brethren, be strong in the Lord, and in the power of his might. Put on the whole armour of God, that ye may be able to stand against *the wiles of the devil.* For we wrestle not against flesh and blood, but against *principalities, against powers, against the rulers of the darkness of this world, against spiritual wickedness in high places.* Wherefore take unto you the whole armour of God, that ye may be able to withstand in the evil day, and having done all, to stand. [The symbolism and terminology used here is unmistakably that of ranked armies.] (italics mine)

*1 Peter 3:21-22:* . . . Jesus Christ: Who is gone into heaven, and is on the right hand of God; angels and *authorities and powers* being made subject unto him. (italics mine)

Ed Murphy quotes the listing, developed by McAlpine in his *New Testament Word Field for Powers,* of the seven Greek words which appear in the verses we've quoted above. These are variously translated by use of the English "ruler," "power," "authority," "throne," "dominion" and "spiritual force." The effect of the words, especially in Ephesians 6, suggests a ranking of power and authority—like an army. Satan himself is called "the prince of the power of the air" in Ephesians 2:2.[6]

Dr. Murphy provides this theological perspective:

> Jesus reveals that Satan directs a mighty kingdom of evil. He has his own evil angels, just as God has His holy angels (Matthew 25:41). Next we discover that these angels are the same as the demon spirits who bind and oppress men (Matthew 12:22-29; Luke 13:10-16; Revelation 12:4-17; 13:1).[7]

Obviously the counter-kingdom is organized. For what purpose?

*Demons are the deadly adversaries of mankind*

Having followed Satan in rebellion, the demons share his murderous, deceiving nature and desire. Their goal is the enslavement and eternal doom of people. They also accuse "the brethren" (God's people by faith), with the obvious desire to see them hurt and harmed.

*Zechariah 3:1:* And he shewed me Joshua the high priest standing before the angel of the LORD, and Satan standing at his right hand *to resist him.* (italics mine)

*Matthew 12:43-45:* [Jesus said] . . . When *the unclean spirit* is gone out of a man, he walketh through dry places, seeking rest, and findeth none. Then he saith, I will return into my house from whence I came out; and when he is come, he findeth it empty, swept, and garnished. Then goeth he, and taketh with himself seven other spirits more wicked than himself, and they enter in and dwell there: and the last state of that man is worse than the first. (italics mine)

*Revelation 12:10:* Now is come salvation, and strength, and the kingdom of our God, and the power of his Christ: for *the accuser of our brethren* is cast down, which accused them before our God day and night. [The rest of the chapter makes it very clear that the entity called the accuser is none other than Satan himself.] (italics mine)

### *Demons want to, and can, possess people*

It is apparent from Scripture that evil spirits want to possess bodies through which they can carry out their wicked activities.

Bible scholars have categorized two levels of demonic impact upon people:

*Demonic oppression*: mild to severe harassment by one or more evil spirits as a result of the opening of some of the gateways to satanic influence.

*Demonic possession*: the condition in which one or more evil spirits actually inhabit the body of a person, taking control of it at will and expressing his (or their) evil personality through the faculties of that human body.[8]

Matthew 12:43-45, as quoted previously, is a classic description of demonic possession; note especially the phrase "they enter in and dwell there." Now consider some of the other Scriptures that describe such possession:

*Matthew 10:1:* And when [Jesus] had called unto him his twelve disciples, he gave them power against unclean spirits, to *cast them out*. (italics mine)

*Mark 5:2-13:* And when [Jesus] was come out of the ship, immediately there met him out of the tombs a man with an unclean spirit, who had his dwelling among the tombs; and no man could bind him, no, not with chains: because that he had been often bound with fetters and chains, and the chains had been plucked asunder by him, and the fetters broken in pieces: neither could any man tame him. And always, night and day, he was in the mountains, and in the tombs, crying, and cutting himself with stones. But when he saw Jesus afar off, he ran and worshipped him, and cried with a loud voice, and said, What have I to do with thee, Jesus, thou Son of the most high God? I adjure thee by God, that thou torment me not. For he said unto him, *Come out of the man, thou unclean spirit.* And [Jesus] asked him, What is thy name? And he answered, saying, My name is Legion: for we are many. And he besought him much that he would not send them away out of the country. Now there was there nigh unto the mountains a great herd of swine feeding. And all the devils besought him, saying, Send us into the swine, that we may *enter into them.* And forthwith Jesus gave them leave. And the unclean spirits went out, and *entered into the swine*: and the herd ran violently down a steep place into the sea, (they were about two thousand;) and were choked in the sea. (italics mine)

*Acts 8:7:* For unclean spirits, crying with loud voice, *came out* of many that were *possessed with them* [during the revival in Samaria, under Philip's preaching]. (italics mine)

*Acts 16:16-18:* And it came to pass, as we [the Apostle Paul and Silas] went to prayer, a certain damsel *possessed with a spirit* of divination met us. . . . The same followed Paul and us, and cried, saying, These men are the servants of the most high God, which show unto us the way of salvation. And this did

she many days. But Paul, being grieved,
turned and said *to the spirit*, I command thee
in the name of Jesus Christ to come out of
her. And he *came out* the same hour. (italics
mine)

Note especially that the demons possessing the
Gadarene demoniac of Mark 5 did not want to be
disembodied. They begged to be allowed, by Jesus, to enter a herd of swine.

### *Demons can prophesy*

The Bible gives several examples of this deceptive demonic activity, such as the account of the
demonized fortune-teller quoted above. There is
also a fascinating passage in First Kings, where the
prophet Micaiah, speaking for the Lord, told a
parable against the false prophets who had predicted success for the wicked king of Israel:

*1 Kings 22:21-22:* . . . there came forth a spirit
. . . and said . . . I will go forth, and I will be
a lying spirit in the mouth of all his prophets.

### *Demons seek the worship of people—*
### *though it is forbidden by God*

Predictably, the worship of Satan and demons
is grotesque, often involving bizarre idolatry, vile
ritualism and human sacrifice—even child sacrifices.

*Leviticus 17:7:* And they shall no more offer their sacrifices unto devils.

*Psalm 106:37-38:* Yea, they sacrificed their sons and daughters unto devils, and shed innocent blood, even the blood of their sons and of their daughters, whom they sacrificed unto the idols of Canaan.

*Revelation 9:20:* And the rest of the men which were not killed by these plagues yet repented not of the works of their hands, that they should not worship devils, and idols of gold, and silver, and brass, and stone, and of wood.

### Demons are predicted to become increasingly active in the closing days of human history

The Bible makes it clear that Satan and his hosts are a defeated army—legally defeated. When Christ died and rose again, He sealed His victory over the enemy. He "led captivity captive" (Ephesians 4:8). Though the sentence was passed on Satan at the cross of Christ and at the empty tomb, it has not yet been executed. But it will be, as the prophetic Scriptures make abundantly evident.

*Revelation 20:10:* And the devil that deceived them was cast into the lake of fire and brimstone, where the beast and the false prophet

are, and shall be tormented day and night
for ever and ever.

Many students of biblical prophecy are convinced that the time for the complete fulfillment
of the awesome end-time events—the rapture, the
return of Christ and other predicted occurrences—is near. (For a more complete consideration of the prophetic scenario see my book
*Apocalypse Next.*)

Obviously Satan knows it, too, and in his de-
luded state, consumed by hatred for God, the servants of God and mankind in general, he and his
hosts become frenetic in their efforts to delude
and destroy people.

The Scriptures are specific in this regard.

*1 Timothy 4:1-3:* Now the Spirit speaketh ex-
pressly, that in the latter times some shall
depart from the faith, giving heed to seduc-
ing spirits, and doctrines of devils; speaking
lies in hypocrisy; having their conscience
seared with a hot iron; forbidding to marry,
and commanding to abstain from meats,
which God hath created to be received with
thanksgiving.

*Revelation 9:3, 11:* And there came out of the
smoke [of the pit] locusts upon the earth:
and unto them was given power. . . . And
they had a king over them, which is the angel of the bottomless pit, whose name in the

Hebrew tongue is Abaddon, but in the Greek tongue hath his name Apollyon [the devil.]

I personally believe that, just as there was massive demonic opposition and activity at the time of Christ's first advent, so there will be greatly increased demonic activity prior to His second coming.

I also believe that, in our time, we are seeing this happen in a myriad of ways—*one* of which is in the UFO explosion.

## UFOnauts Surely Do Look Like Demons

Certainly the UFOnauts behave in a way which the Scriptures we have considered say demons act.

- UFOnauts are apparently ranked, as their channelled messages clearly indicate.
- UFOnauts profess peace and prosperity (they say they're benevolent), but the things they do to people discredit such claims.
- UFOnauts seek to possess people. The UFO literature is *full* of the accounts of such possessions. Whitley Strieber's personal account is chillingly graphic:

I became entirely given over to extreme dread. The fear was so powerful that it seemed to make my personality completely evaporate. . . . "Whitley" ceased to exist. What was left was a body and a state of raw fear so

great that it swept about me like a thick, suffo-
cating curtain, turning paralysis into a condition that seemed close to death. . . .

I had been captured like a wild animal on
December 26 . . . rendered helpless. . . . They
had changed me, done something to me. . . . I
wondered if I might not be in the grip of demons.[9]

- UFOnauts want the devotion and obedience of
  human beings, whom they seek to control.
- UFOnauts prophesy—in both senses of the
  word. They foretell the future and they give
  messages. Medicine Grizzlybear Lake's experience, mentioned in chapter 8, comes to mind.
- And, as also noted in chapter 8, UFOnauts are
  increasingly in evidence, in unprecedented
  numbers. If indeed the greatly increased activity of UFOs and the demonic is another sign,
  among many, of prophetic fulfillment—as I
  believe it is—this should spur us to action
  spiritually.

In part four we'll consider what spiritual action
we should take, according to the Bible, to avoid
the UFO trap. Or, for those who may have already been ensnared, we'll describe how to escape
the trap—and in any event be ready for the return
of Christ.

Part Four

# Invasion
# or
# Protection?

If indeed, as we have attempted to show, UFOs are real and demonic, what is the wise response?

Particularly, if what is predicted in this book is an accurate reading of the prophetic Scriptures, and the UFO/demonic presence on earth does continue to dramatically increase, how should we respond to this danger?

The choice is really between potential personal pervasion or permanent protection.

Chapters 11 and 12 explore the pathway to protection.

CHAPTER ELEVEN

# *Avoiding the Trap*

As we have documented from Scripture and the representative experiences of individuals, Satan and his demons have as their diabolical goal the entrapment, enslavement and eternal doom of mankind.

They are a fearsome multifaceted foe.

They have very real power.

They are deceptive and implacable.

They are more than a match for us in our own human strength.

But there's a guaranteed way to be to be assured of safety. That way is to genuinely give oneself to God, becoming His child through faith in the Lord Jesus Christ, and then walking close to Him in obedience to His Word.

## Become a Child of God

Step one is to find Christ. The Bible makes it

abundantly clear that a personal relationship with the Lord Jesus Christ is essential to becoming a child of God.

It is not enough to be born into a "Christian" nation or a Christian family. Each person must individually and personally, by an act of the will, enter into a relationship with God through Christ.

The Bible declares that *all* mankind is in one of two spiritual families, which are headed by either God or Satan. By nature and by choice all of us are sinners. Because we have come short of the standard of God's holiness, *every one* of us, through natural birth, is spiritually in the family of Satan (Romans 3:23).

Jesus said to some extremely religious, very moral people, "Ye are of your father the devil" (John 8:44). This doesn't mean that those people, or that unconverted people generally, are necessarily devilish, evil or terrible persons.

It *does* mean that because of our by-natural-birth sin nature, we are separated from God, and therefore related spiritually, not to God, but to Satan.

The solution is to have a spiritual birth, to receive new life from and through Christ. The Bible says, in John 1:12-13:

> But as many as received him [Christ], to them gave he power to *become the sons of God,* even to them that believe on his name: which were born, not of blood, nor of the will of the flesh, nor of the will of man, but of God. [italics mine]

This verse is clearly describing the spiritual act of becoming a child of God on the basis of being born of God.

Jesus said to a religious leader—an upright, moral, good man—"Except a man be born again, he cannot see the kingdom of God. . . . Ye must be born again" (John 3:3, 7).

That leader, Nicodemus by name, was confused. How could he be born when he was already old? But Jesus explained that He was not talking about physical birth, but rather about *spiritual birth*.

And spiritual birth happens as a person takes what I call the "ABC" steps, which mean "Agree," "Believe" and "Call."

### First: Agree

Agree with God in all that He says in His Word, the Bible, about the fact that you are separated from God by your sinful nature and sinful actions. Admit that you have broken God's laws and come short of His holy standard.

Agree with God that sin deserves His punishment because He is a just, holy and righteous God. Admit that you are properly under that sentence and that you deserve it completely.

The Bible makes these facts very clear:

For all have sinned, and come short of the glory [standard] of God. (Romans 3:23)

[God's] eyes are too pure to look on evil;

[He] cannot tolerate wrong. (Habakkuk 1:13, NIV)

Nothing impure will ever enter it [heaven], nor will anyone who does what is shameful or deceitful. (Revelation 21:27, NIV)

For the wages of sin is death. (Romans 6:23)

The Bible describes three kinds of death: *physical* death (the state experienced when life leaves our bodies); *spiritual* death (the spiritual separation from God caused by our sinful nature and behavior; a person thus can be alive physically but dead spiritually [Ephesians 2:1]); and *eternal* death (the fixed state of separation from God entered into by the individual who dies physically while he is still dead spiritually).

It is eternal death, in particular, which is the horrible result of sin. The Lord Jesus Christ frequently described such a death as being eternal (without end) in a destiny which He called hell. He described hell as a literal place of judgment (Matthew 13:42), a place of everlasting fire (Matthew 18:8), a place of torment (Luke 16:24, 28), a place of wailing and gnashing of teeth (Matthew 13:50), a place of bitter memory (Luke 16:25) and a place originally prepared for the devil and his angels (Matthew 25:41). In fact, Jesus more often warned about hell than He spoke about heaven. It is not God's will or desire that any person should be consigned to perish eternally in hell (2 Peter 3:9), but rather that all should come to repentance.

God's justice, however, requires that "The soul who sins is the one who will die" (Ezekiel 18:4, NIV).

So, agree with God, admitting that you are a sinner under His just condemnation for your sin and that you are in need of His salvation.

## Second: Believe

Next, believe that God does not want you to perish eternally in the torment of hell because of your sin. Believe that God loves you so much that He provided a way whereby He could still be just, holy and righteous—and yet pardon you, a sinner.

Believe that God did not merely overlook sin, but that He sent His only begotten Son, the Lord Jesus Christ, to provide salvation by personally and fully paying the penalty for sin. Jesus did that by dying—as the perfect, sinless God-man—as our substitute to pay for our sin.

Believe that Jesus Christ, whose life, death, burial and resurrection is the best-attested fact of all antiquity,[1] did come to earth to live, die, rise again and ascend to heaven in order to provide a life that never ends for all who trust Him.

Believe that Jesus Christ, and He alone, can save you because He has fully satisfied the just demands of a holy God. Believe that you can't become righteous in God's sight in any other way—particularly not by any of your own effort.

Believe that Christ *wants* to save you and that He *will* save you.

The Bible provides a solid basis for such belief:

> The Lord is not slack concerning his promise . . . but is longsuffering to [us], not willing that any should perish, but that all should come to repentance. (2 Peter 3:9)

> For God so loved the world, that he gave his only begotten Son, that whosoever believeth in him should not perish, but have everlasting life. (John 3:16)

> But God commendeth his love toward us, in that, while we were yet sinners, Christ died for us. (Romans 5:8)

> Being justified freely by his grace through the redemption that is in Christ Jesus: whom God hath set forth to be a propitiation [atonement] through faith in his blood, to declare his righteousness for the remission of sins that are past, through the forbearance of God; to declare . . . his righteousness: that he might be just, and the justifier of him which believeth in Jesus. (Romans 3:24-26)

> Moreover, brethren, I declare unto you the gospel . . . how that Christ died for our sins . . . that he was buried, and that he rose

again the third day according to the scriptures. (1 Corinthians 15:1,3-4)

Neither is there salvation in any other: for there is none other name under heaven given among men, whereby we must be saved. (Acts 4:12)

[Jesus said], "I am the way and the truth and the life. No one comes to the Father except through me." (John 14:6, NIV)

All that the Father giveth me shall come to me; and him that cometh to me I will in no wise cast out. (John 6:37)

### *Third: Come and Call*

It is not enough to agree with God that you have a need and believe that Christ can and will save you.

You must act upon those facts.

You must repent of sin. That is, you must be sorry for your sin, sorry enough to completely turn from it and from your own efforts, or any other hope. You must come to Christ, calling upon Him for salvation and counting on the fact that He will do what He has promised. This means simply taking, by faith, the gift of pardon and eternal life which He offers.

Merely believing intellectually about Jesus Christ without coming to Him makes as much sense, and is as effective, as believing that a medication can successfully treat a fatal disease, but failing to take it!

Again, the Bible provides the basis for such statements:

> He that believeth on the Son hath everlasting life: and he that believeth not the Son shall not see life; but the wrath of God abideth on him. (John 3:36)

> He that believeth on him [Jesus Christ] is not condemned: but he that believeth not is condemned already, because he hath not believed in the name of the only begotten Son of God. (John 3:18)

It is important to note that the Greek word translated "believe" in the above verses means to "rest one's entire weight and trust on the object or person in which the belief is placed." It requires action in keeping with the intellectual assent of that belief.

> Whosoever shall call upon the name of the Lord shall be saved. (Romans 10:13)

> [T]he gift of God is eternal life through Jesus Christ our Lord. (Romans 6:23)

The logical question you may be asking at this point is: How do I come to Christ and call upon

Him? Do I have to go to a church or some religious leader to do so? No.

"Calling upon the Lord" is just another term for praying or talking to God. To talk to God is not a complicated process, dependent upon some special person, place or rituals. God has invited people to approach Him, through His Son, in simple, straightforward terms. In fact, Jesus spoke approvingly of the approach of the despised tax collector who simply prayed, "God, be merciful to me, a sinner."

While the exact words of your prayer to God are not of vital importance (since God sees and knows the attitude of your heart), the following is the kind of prayer that you could pray in calling upon God for salvation:

> *Dear Lord Jesus: I realize that I need You. I admit that I have sinned and that I deserve Your just, eternal punishment for that sin. But I am sorry for my sins and sincerely willing to turn from them. I believe that You died and rose again to pay sin's penalty on my behalf. I come to You and open my heart to You. I ask You to come into my life, forgive me for all my sin, cleanse me from it and make me Your child. I invite You to take control of my life and to cause me to be the kind of person that You want me to be.*
>
> *I thank You for doing this—because You have promised that whoever calls upon You, as I have now done, will be saved. I pray this in the name of the Son of God, the Lord Jesus Christ. Amen.*

If this prayer expresses the true desire of your heart, I urge you to sincerely express it to God as *your* prayer.

Then, once you have prayed, *tell someone* what you have done. The Bible says that when we believe on the Lord Jesus Christ in our heart, God forgives our sin and counts us righteous, and that when we openly confess with our mouth what we have believed in our heart, God gives us assurance of that salvation (Romans 10:9-10).

## Walk Close to Christ

A birth is not the end; it's the beginning. And when a person is born again, it's the start of a new spiritual life. That life is intended to be one of walking close to Christ in obedience to Him. It involves taking time, on a daily basis, to read God's Word and talk to Him in prayer.

It is also a life intended to be lived corporately. Find a local church where the pastor and people believe and teach the Bible and where they are committed to obeying God in the power which He gives by His Holy Spirit. Make a practice of regular attendance at such a church.

The ability to walk closely with Christ is, in fact, beyond our natural ability. It requires that we be filled with His Spirit.

## Be Filled with the Spirit

In a nutshell, to be filled with the Holy Spirit is to invite Him (He is a *Person*) to take charge of your life.

Just as simply as you would invite a friend into your home, you can in sincerity say to God the Holy Spirit, "I invite You to take charge of my life. Lead me, guide me, teach me, make me into the person You want me to be."

He will supernaturally produce in you, as you yield to Him, the characteristics (the Bible calls them "fruit") of the Spirit: love, joy, peace, patience, kindness, goodness, faithfulness, gentleness and self-control.

## Follow the Lord

The Holy Spirit will certainly lead you to engage in those activities that will cause you to grow in your spiritual life. As already alluded to, these will include daily ingesting the spiritual food of God's Word; the fresh air of prayer—talking to God; the practice of regular fellowship with a church that honors and obeys God's Word and sharing with others your commitment to Christ.

Please note that we do not engage in these spiritual exercises in an effort to obtain salvation. Salvation is a free gift from God. However, we do the above in order to grow and follow the Lord.

## Stand against the Foe

It is also important in your relationship to Christ and your life lived under the control of the Holy Spirit that you join the battle against the enemy. That means to put on what the Bible calls "the armor of God."

Put on the whole armour of God, that ye may
be able to stand against the wiles of the devil.
For we wrestle not against flesh and blood,
but against principalities, against powers,
against the rulers of the darkness of this
world, against spiritual wickedness in high
places. Wherefore take unto you the whole armour of God, that ye may be able to withstand in the evil day, and having done all, to
stand. Stand therefore, having your loins girt
about with truth, and having on the breast-
plate of righteousness; and your feet shod
with the preparation of the gospel of peace;
above all, taking the shield of faith, wherewith
ye shall be able to quench all the fiery darts of
the wicked. And take the helmet of salvation,
and the sword of the Spirit, which is the word
of God: praying always with all prayer and
supplication in the Spirit, and watching there-
unto with all perseverance and supplication
for all saints. (Ephesians 6:11-18)

So here are the key elements of knowing God
personally and (as a by-product) of avoiding the
enemy's trap:

- Find Christ.
- Be filled with the Spirit.
- Follow the Lord.
- Stand against the foe.

May this be your experience!

What I have written in *UFOs: Friend, Foe or Fantasy?* is not intended to suggest that *every* person who has not yet been born again will be demonized or be in danger of UFO abduction. However, it *is* intended to mean that the person who *is* born again, filled with the Spirit, following the Lord and standing against the foe by fleeing evil *will* be blessedly free of the enemy's enslavement and ultimate doom.

To personally know Christ as Savior and Lord: it's life's most important, most essential, decision.

# CHAPTER TWELVE

## *Escaping the Trap*

Perhaps you've realized, as you've read to this point, that you have—to some degree or other—been entrapped by Satan. Or you may know someone, friend or relative, whom you feel may have fallen into the enemy's snare.

Maybe you have opened, in your life, some of the doorways to the demonic as described in chapter 9, and have sensed that the enemy has, in fact, entered. You may even have had an abduction experience.

Perhaps you've lost control to entities in your life that frighten you, as you find yourself compelled to do things you can't understand and don't want to be doing.

And you want out.

Or, if it's a relative or friend about whom you're concerned, you'd like to have some idea about how to help them. If this is your situation, become familiar with the directions given here and communicate these principles to the one for whom you are concerned. A word of caution is in order, however. Should you encounter a situation with which you are unfamiliar and are uncertain of how to proceed, it would be wise to seek the counsel and help of a mature Christian, such as a pastor or qualified counselor.

## There Is a Way Out

There is a way to escape Satan's trap. While it is not as easy as falling off a log, it isn't complex or difficult to understand.

1. The way out begins by becoming a child of God through faith in Christ, as detailed in chapter 11. If you've not yet done so, sincerely take the "ABC steps" now. And the key word is *sincerely*. Acknowledging your need, repenting of sin and trusting the Lord Jesus Christ for salvation must not be viewed as just a means to an end—in order to be free of satanic intrusion into your life. You must be genuine and sincere in coming to God with a desire to become a part of His "forever family."

If you have opened doorways into your life, coming to Christ for salvation involves for you (as an essential part of your repentance for sin) a definite, deliberate renouncing of *all* of your involvement in the occult, New Age, demonic and related entanglements.

You absolutely must sever all such contacts and turn completely from all such activities.

Every one of your occult objects, pictures, videos, tapes, CDs, books, pornography and so on
*must* be COMPLETELY DESTROYED—preferably by
burning, if possible. There is a biblical precedent for such a seemingly extreme action. In the
book of Acts, the newly converted believers who
had practiced sorcery publicly burned their
books of magic arts (19:18-20).

2. In connection with the destruction of all occult
   paraphernalia verbally renounce any and all
   connections to the occult. Acknowledge that
   such activities are sin, and specifically claim the
   covering of Christ's atoning blood over your
   past occult sins (Revelation 12:11; 1 John 1:9).

You should pray in this fashion:

*I confess that my involvement with* _____
*is sin. I repent of it and by an act of my will I re-
nounce all such involvement. I ask You, Lord Jesus
Christ, to forgive me and to cleanse me in Your
atoning blood. I pray in the strong name of the
Lord Jesus Christ.*

By verbally declaring that your past occult involvement was sin, that you repent of it and are
severing all ties to it, you serve notice on the enemy that, by a deliberate act of your will, you are
turning from service and enslavement to him in
order to trust and serve Christ. There is spiritual
power in such a declaration.

3. It is also important to fully forgive any who may have wronged you in the past. An unforgiving spirit short-circuits a relationship with Christ (Matthew 18:22). Such forgiveness may be extremely difficult to extend—particularly if the offenses have been grievous. Simply ask God, through Christ, to give you the ability to forgive—to roll over onto God the responsibility for dealing with the offender(s).

4. Rebellion is another issue. The Bible says that "rebellion is as the sin of witchcraft" (1 Samuel 15:23). It was the sin of Satan that led to his expulsion from heaven (Ezekiel 28:12-17). If there are persons in your life who have had legitimate authority over you—against whom you have rebelled—you must deal with that sin. Confess it to God, and accept His forgiveness. Then acknowledge it to the one(s) against whom you have rebelled (most often parents), seek forgiveness and where appropriate, depending on your age and situation, get back under that authority. Do so even if the authority figure isn't a Christian. You need to accept their authority except, of course, in cases where their direction is in conflict with God's Word.

5. Then, having taken the above steps, in the name of the Lord Jesus Christ, command every one of the forces of evil to get out of your life and go to the abyss. It is important to command in His full, threefold name: the

Lord Jesus Christ. His name is the name above every name, and there is unlimited power in the name of Jesus (Galatians 2:20; Ephesians 1:19-22, 2:5-6; Philippians 2:9-11).

6. Another important step to take is to be certain to invite the Holy Spirit to come and live in you and to be in control of you. All believers have the Holy Spirit, but that is a far cry from allowing Him to have complete control. He is the Spirit of love, of wisdom and truth, and you can completely trust Him. With the Holy Spirit filling your spirit there will be no room for any of the dark spirits to have any part of you. Make a sincere commitment to read God's Word and to pray on a daily basis. Determine to become part of a Bible-believing church (1 Peter 2:2; 1 Thessalonians 5:17; Colossians 4:2; Hebrews 10:24-25).

Should you encounter difficulties in ridding your life of the demonic on your own, it may be that you are missing some aspect of your past which needs to be renounced or some similar facet of the spiritual struggle. You may need help in dealing fully with the matters of forgiveness and past rebellion. If such a situation should occur, it would be good to seek the help of a mature brother or sister in Christ, as suggested above. A wise, spiritually sensitive and mature believer can often provide the objectivity and the support which may be needed. And after all, the family of

God is intended by our Father to "be there" for one another.

Foster has a very significant comment which has bearing on this matter:

> If, for example, a victim of invasion can be led to say, "I, in the name of the Lord Jesus Christ, refuse and repudiate and renounce this spirit of _____, and I cast it out of my life, into the abyss, in the name of the Lord Jesus Christ," that victim may well find release, on the basis of his/her deontic [morally binding] authority, but if there is appreciable or extensive bondage, very, very often the individuals are not physically able to make verbal renunciations such as the one described. Victims who effect their own deliverance through guided verbalizations do so on the basis of believers' authority—their own.[1]

It has been our experience in our limited involvement in exorcism, that songs of praise to the Lord Jesus Christ, particularly those that speak of His shed blood for our atonement, have great power in defeating the foe. The reading aloud of God's Word is also a formidable weapon to use against the enemy, since Satan and all his hosts hate the praise of God, especially musical, and the Word of God.

In addition, I recommend the books *The Bondage Breaker* and *Victory over the Darkness*, by Neil Anderson (listed in the bibliography at the back of this book).

It would also be wise to be in contact with a local pastor who believes the Bible to be God's Word, who preaches the message of salvation through Christ alone, who is aware of the spiritual warfare between the forces of Satan and of God and who knows how to see the enemy defeated through the power of Christ. As was outlined in chapter 11, it is vitally important that Christians be part of a local body of believers, and a church with a spiritual leader such as we've profiled here is one that will give the kind of ongoing support that will be a blessing to you.

God bless you.

## Responding to "Chance" Encounters

Even though UFO experiences come primarily to non-Christians, Christians are not completely immune from demonic attack, as indicated earlier. What if such a UFO contact occurs?

Suppose you are driving down a highway and a "spacecraft" approaches your vehicle. Or maybe you are out for a stroll in the evening and you see an unusual object in a field, or you are approached by beings that appear to be "extraterrestrial."

In light of our thesis that UFO abductions are demonic, what action should you take?

There are a variety of "anti-alien" devices advertised in some of the UFO magazines that claim to offer protection. They range from relatively inexpensive "no aliens" stickers to equipment costing hundreds of dollars—all of which purport to repel any alien approach!

But such devices will *not* protect against evil spirits. Therefore, UFO encounters must be resisted in the same way as any other demonic attack. The response needs to be a simple pronouncement: "I resist and rebuke you in the name and authority of the Lord Jesus Christ. I command you to go where Jesus sends you."

David Fessenden, my editor, met a fellow author at Sandy Cove Writers' Conference in 1995 who had just such an experience. This Christian woman described how one night she was awakened from a sound sleep. She saw an alien-like entity in her bedroom and felt a foreboding sense of evil. Instinctively, she called out to the Lord and rebuked the apparition in the name of Jesus. The entity vanished!

There *is* authority and power in His Name!

---

If you have prayed to receive the Lord Jesus Christ as Savior while reading *UFOs: Friend, Foe or Fantasy?*, I would be grateful to know of your decision and will be happy to respond with suggestions for growth in your new Christian life. Kindly address me at:

Pastor Bill
3825 Hartzdale Drive
Camp Hill, PA 17011

# APPENDIX A

One of the most controversial passages of Scripture is a portion which many feel may have a direct bearing on the current UFO flap—particularly in relationship to the sexual aspect of most of the purported abductions.

The passage is Genesis 6:1-4, which reads:

> And it came to pass, when men began to multiply on the face of the earth, and daughters were born unto them, that the sons of God saw the daughters of men that they were fair; and they took them wives of all which they chose. And the LORD said, My spirit shall not always strive with man, for that he also is flesh: yet his days shall be an hundred and twenty years. There were giants in the earth in those days; and also after that, when the sons of God came in unto the daughters of men, and they bare children to them, the same became mighty men which were of old, men of renown.

The questions that arise are these: "According to this Scripture, did fallen angels (demons) have sexual relations with human women?" and secondly, "If in fact, Genesis 6:1-4 does indicate this, could the bizarre present-day abduction accounts of UFOnaut rapes or sexual encounters aboard spaceships be the same thing?"

Many have speculated that the answer to one or both of these questions is in the affirmative.[1] Proponents of such a view generally also accept the existence and nefarious activity of the *incubi* (male demons who rape sleeping women) and the *succubi* (female demons who seduce men). That such theories have a very long history in the annals of mankind cannot be denied.

Nor can the debased preoccupation with sex demonstrated by Satan and his hosts be discounted. In chapter 9 we documented the fact that illicit sexual activity is indeed a doorway for the demonization of individuals.

As indicated earlier, the Genesis passage is controversial, with little neutrality in the interpretation or understanding of it. And wide indeed is the range of interpretations!

The two most common viewpoints are:

One: Women and demonic beings ("sons of God"—a term often used in Scripture to refer to angels) had sexual relations. Their mutant offspring, part human and part demon, were said to be the Nephilim, the "heroes of old"—giants of superhuman proportions.

Two: The "sons of God" who consorted with the daughters of men were human descendants of the *godly* line of Seth, while the women were from the *ungodly* line of Cain. Because of this "unequal yoke," civilization became depraved to the point that, in the Flood, God subsequently destroyed all but the righteous Noah and his immediate family.

An array of Bible scholars can be marshalled in support of each of these interpretations.

Hugh Ross, of *Reasons to Believe*, in a position paper entitled "Sons of God . . . Who Are They?" summarizes his view that they are demonic by writing:

> [S]ince the term "sons of God' in Genesis 6:2 and 6:4 is in the time context of after the fall of man and before the resurrection of Jesus Christ, this would indicate it refers to demons and not to men. . . . Also, the earthly descendants of the sons of God, the Nephilim (alias Rephaim, Anakim, Anakites, giants), were at least occasionally of superhuman dimensions. Goliath, for example, was at least 9'9" tall, which exceeds by nine inches the maximum possible height for effective mobility by human beings. Moreover, studies of demonic encounters indicate that many, if not most, demons are intensely preoccupied with illicit sex.[2]

Chuck Missler expounds the same view, extending it to embrace the possibility that the reported

UFO implantation and harvesting of fetuses could be a similar activity of the fallen angels, currently masquerading as UFOnauts.

In a taped lecture entitled "The Return of the Nephilim," Missler maintains that the original Hebrew language in Genesis 6 always refers to angels, while the Hebrew for the "daughters of men" means daughters of Adam—not Cain. He says that Nephilim means "fallen ones" in the original, and that these were also called "mighty ones."

As do others, Missler refers to Jude 6-7 and Second Peter 2:4 in support of his view:

> *Jude 6-7*: And the angels which kept not their first estate, but left their own habitation, he hath reserved in everlasting chains under darkness unto the judgment of the great day. Even as Sodom and Gomorrah, and the cities about them in like manner, giving themselves over to fornication, and going after strange flesh, are set forth for an example, suffering the vengeance of eternal fire.

> *2 Peter 2:4*: For if God spared not the angels that sinned, but cast them down to hell, and delivered them into chains of darkness, to be reserved unto judgment.

He also notes that this view was widely held among the ancients: Jewish rabbis and historians as well as numerous leaders of the early Church.[3]

In *Powers of Darkness*, Arnold Clinton discusses the fact that many Jewish writers interpreted the Genesis 6 reference to "the sons of God" as being angels (called "Watchers") who rebelled against God. The Jewish apocryphal book First Enoch devotes thirty-one chapters to the account of this fall. The dark angels, according to this record, taught mankind many evil arts, and their offspring were freakish giants.[4]

I.D.E. Thomas, author of the highly speculative *The Omega Conspiracy*, accepts the theory that the Nephilim were fallen angels who came to earth to commit carnal acts with human women. The result, according to Thomas, was the near annihilation of the race through genetic impurity, but God flooded the earth, sparing only Noah and his family, and imprisoned the evil spirits.[5]

He speculates that demonic entities could be working in these last days, using UFOs, to conquer the world and bring in the Antichrist through a super-race.

Numerous other writers who hold to this first-mentioned interpretation could be cited.

## But There's Another View

On the other hand, a great many authors and Bible teachers accept the second interpretation which we've described.

Clifford Wilson, who, through his best-sellers *Crash Go the Chariots* and *The Chariots Still Crash*, thoroughly debunked the bizarre ideas put forward in Eric Von Daniken's *Chariots of the Gods*, considers the first viewpoint a possibility, but opts for the second interpretation as being more plausible.[6] (Von Daniken, and more recently Zecharia Sitchin, claim aliens created humans through genetic experiments with animals—just one of a great many completely unsupported theories.)

Bible teacher Dr. J. Sidlow Baxter in *Studies in Problem Texts* writes:

> Angels are bodiless, purely spiritual beings, and sexless. Being bodiless and sexless means that they are without sex organs, and that they are therefore absolutely incapable of sensuous experiences or sexual processes; nor are they capable of procreation or reproduction in any way whatever.[7]

Though not mentioned specifically by Baxter, the words of the Lord Jesus Christ come to mind: "[The angels] neither marry, nor are given in marriage" (Matthew 22:30).

Gleason Archer, author of *Encyclopedia of Bible Difficulties*, calls the Genesis account "the first recorded occurrence of mixed marriage between believers and unbelievers," with its attendant tragic results, morally and spiritually. He believes the two groups were descendants of Seth and Cain respectively.[8]

I personally find the response of Hank Hanegraaff, Christian Research Institute president, best-selling author and host of the syndicated radio show "The Bible Answer Man," to be the most satisfying answer to this difficult question.

Hanegraaff accepts the Sethian/Cainian interpretation and outlines seven reasons why he does so:

1. He agrees with Baxter that demons are non-material, nonsexual beings, and therefore incapable of producing biological offspring.

2. He points out that if demonic sexual relations with human beings and the subsequent procreation occurred in ancient times, there would be no way of precluding it now, and no assurance that the people we meet today are fully human.

3. Hanegraaff shows that the term "Nephilim" was used in the description of some who were part of an event that occurred 800 years *after* the Flood (Numbers 13:33). Thus, if the mutant theory is accepted, either not all supposed mutants perished in the Flood (contrary to scriptural testimony), or mutants were produced after the Flood—which would give a biblical precedent to expect such to be produced today.

4. The first chapter of Genesis makes it clear that God's creation was designed to reproduce "according to their *own* kind." This leaves no place for mutants.

5. Hanegraaff says that the Bible reveals the Flood to be a judgment solely on mankind, not a judgment on fallen angels or mutants.

6. The mutant theory raises serious questions about the spiritual accountability of the supposed mutants, and of their relationship to redemption. Hanegraaff points out that the angels rebelled and are judged individually, with no redemption offered to them. By contrast, man fell and is judged corporately, in Adam, and has had redemption made available corporately in Christ. There is no category in Scripture for the demon-human.

7. While the passages in First Peter 3:19-20, Second Peter 2:4 and Jude 6-7 do seem to be consistent with a mutant theory, they do not necessitate or establish the theory. Moreover, says Hanegraaff, the term "sons of God"—when used of angels—is explicitly applied to *good* angels (Job 1:6; 2:1; 38:7; Psalm 29:1; 89:6-7). He quotes Archer who writes:

> The term "sons of God' (*bene elohim* transliterated from Hebrew) is used in the Old Testament of either angels or men who are true believers, committed to the service of God.[9]

Hanegraaff also observes that the term "giants" in Genesis 6 is more often translated from the Hebrew by the words "men of renown."[10]

While the questions are admittedly difficult to answer, the Seth/Cain-line response is, in my judgment, less speculative about a matter on which the Scripture is basically silent, and more in line with what the Bible does clearly reveal.

And, if indeed there were no demonic/human sexual relationships which produced mutant offspring in earth's earliest ages, there is no reason to believe that the demonic/UFOnaut entities can produce such today.

The purported pregnancies, births and displays of mutant fetuses reported by abductees must therefore be simply demonic deceptions. Powerful and persuasive, undoubtedly, but deceptions nonetheless.

## APPENDIX B

Occult contacts with "spirit guides" and angelic beings bear a striking resemblance to the messages and manifestations of UFOnauts. One example of this is the popular book, *The Messengers: A True Story of Angelic Presence and the Return to the Age of Miracles*. It sounds like an appealing volume, a welcome addition to the growing genre of angel books.

It is, however, a New Age book which specifically contradicts virtually every major tenet of orthodox Christian doctrine. As such, it is fairly typical of the majority of New Age writings.

It is, as well, almost a carbon copy of the main messages coming from the UFOnauts—which is certainly not a surprising fact.

*The Messengers* purports to be the account of "angelic" visitations to, and guidance of, a Portland, Oregon businessman. It includes the transcript of the account of his "previous incarnation as the Apostle Paul," a record obtained under regression hypnosis!

Another similarity to the UFO experience is seen in the sudden appearance to the businessman, at one point, of "three huge bands of orange-gold light" which then zoomed toward the contactee, stopping directly above where he stood. The lights appeared to grow larger over a brief period of time, then later disappeared.

A similar band of light is predicted by the angels to encircle the entire globe as a part of future dramatic and major spiritual events before the year 2000.[1]

All of this (which has resulted in the July 1997 printing of 350,000 hard-cover copies of *The Messengers*, following a self-published soft-cover edition) began with a visit to a psychic who, from a trance, gave the guidance which started the man on his journey of deception.

The book, through the hypnotic recovery of the "preexistent life and statements" of the businessman—as "Paul"—contradicts not only the biblical record of Paul's New Testament writings and the historical account of his life, but—as indicated above—every major tenet of the historic Christian faith.

Among the numerous contradictions are these:

We're all sons and daughters of God. We all are and we all have God inside us. A part of God.[2]

God and nature are one.[3]

He [Jesus] is not a unique Son of God, but a son of God more in touch [than others] with the God within him.[4]

God does not judge or punish sin.[5]

Jesus did not believe in the resurrection of the body, but rather in reincarnation.[6]

*The Messengers* contains numerous other contradictions of biblical doctrine, as well as errors of historical fact. But the significance of this book is the striking similarity of its theology to the UFOnaut messages. This similarity is yet another confirmation of the fact that these entities oppose, either stridently or subtly, the biblical revelation of God, His character, the deity of Jesus Christ, the means of salvation, the principles of godly spiritual life and so much more.

Such entities, whether they appear as superintelligent extraterrestrials or heavenly angels, are unquestionably from the counter-kingdom, and as such are the bitter, dangerous, deadly enemies of God and mankind. In Second Corinthians 11:12-15 the real Apostle Paul describes deceitful false apostles and says that such things are no surprise, for Satan himself masquerades as an angel of light. It is not surprising then, if his servants masquerade as servants of righteousness.

# ENDNOTES

## Part One

1 *The Patriot News,* Harrisburg, PA, June 8, 1996, religion section, 2. A 1996 Religion News Service poll by Ohio University and Scripps-Howard News Service indicated that fifty percent of Americans believe that flying saucers are real and that there is a government cover-up.

2 A 1973 Christian Research Institute cassette recording by Dr. Walter Martin quoted a then-current Gallup poll in which fifty-one percent said they believed UFOs were real, and over 15 million U.S. residents claimed to have seen one.

## Chapter One

1 Jacques Vallee, *Dimensions: A Casebook of Alien Contact* (Chicago: Contemporary Books, 1988), 9.

2 Keith Thompson, *Angels and Aliens* (New York: Fawcett Columbine, 1991), 119.

3 Vallee, *Dimensions,* 10-12.

4 W. Raymond Drake, *Gods and Spacemen in the Ancient East* (New York: Signet Books, 1968), chapters 3-14.

5 Andrew Tomas, *We Are Not the First* (New York: Bantam Books, 1973), 99-110.

6 *UFOs: The Hidden Truth* video (New Liberty Films and Videos), n.d.

7 Vallee, *Dimensions,* 13.

8 *The UFO Phenomenon* (Alexandria, VA: Time-Life Books, 1987), 69.

[9] Elizabeth Hilstrom, *Testing the Spirits* (Downers Grove, IL: InterVarsity, 1995), 199.

[10] Thompson, *Angels and Aliens,* 3-4.

[11] Vallee, *Dimensions,* 38.

[12] Jacques Vallee, *Passport to Magonia* (Chicago: Contemporary Books, 1993), 213-249.

[13] Associated Press release, July 8, 1947, as quoted in Thompson, *Angels and Aliens,* 1.

[14] Thompson, *Angels and Aliens,* 3.

[15] *The UFO Phenomenon,* 20-22.

[16] Thompson, *Angels and Aliens,* 3.

[17] Vallee, *Dimensions,* 174.

[18] Ibid., 175-178.

[19] *Roswell Daily Record,* July 8, 1947, 1, as quoted in Kevin D. Randle and Donald R. Schmitt, *The Truth About the UFO Crash at Roswell* (New York: Avon Books, 1994), 56.

[20] Randle and Schmitt, *The Truth About the UFO Crash at Roswell*, 3-10. Ragsdale's testimony has been called into some degree of question because of the fact, according to author Kevin Randle's May 1997 America Online letter, that in 1994 he apparently signed an exclusive deal with certain businessmen and for financial inducements is now telling a different story.

Randle concludes that what he considers an important part of the Roswell case is now suspect, in spite of the fact that the original story, basically unaltered, was told and retold by Ragsdale to family members and others over a period of more than forty years prior to the 1994 "financial deal." Randle believes that the deal involves "coaching" as to what Ragsdale should now say. The fiftieth anniversary Roswell crash celebration in July 1997 was seen as a commercial factor in the entire episode.

[21] Ibid., 11-28.

[22] Ibid., 31-63.

23 "The Roswell Incident," Discovery Channel program, November 18, 1995.

## Chapter Two

1 Jerome Clark, *The UFO Files* (Lincolnwood, IL: Public International, 1986), 40-41; Brad Steiger, *Project Blue Book* (New York: Ballantine, 1990), 57-58.

2 Thompson, *Angels and Aliens*, 22.

3 John Weldon, *UFOs: What on Earth Is Happening?* (New York: Bantam Books, 1976), 38-40; Thompson, *Angels and Aliens*, 23-25.

4 *The UFO Phenomenon*, 23.

5 Ibid., 97; Vallee, *Dimensions*, 122-123.

6 J. Allen Hynek, *The UFO Experience: A Scientific Inquiry* (Chicago: Henry Regnery Company, 1972), insert; Thompson, *Angels and Aliens*, 51-54.

7 John G. Fuller, *The Interrupted Journey* (New York: Berkley Medallion Books, 1966).

8 John G. Fuller, *Incident at Exeter* (New York: Berkley Medallion Books, 1966).

9 *The UFO Phenomenon*, 119.

10 Jenny Randles and Peter Hough, *The World's Best "True" UFO Stories* (New York: Sterling Publishers Company, Inc. 1994), 14-16.

11 Clark, *The UFO Files*, 80.

12 Thompson, *Angels and Aliens*, 103-105.

13 Warren Smith, *The Book of Encounters* (New York: Zebra Books, 1976), 70-86.

14 Randles and Hough, *The World's Best*, 63-66.

15 Ibid., 90-95.

16 Jacques Vallee, *Confrontations: A Scientist's Search for Alien Contact* (New York: Ballantine, 1990), 173-194.

[17] *The UFO Phenomenon,* 50-51.

[18] Nelson Pacheco and Tommy Blann, *Unmasking the Enemy* (Arlington, VA: Bendan Press, 1994), 205-232, 239-263.

[19] Ibid., 234. The most dramatic example among the dozen or so which they cite is that of Holly Maddux, whose blood-drained and mutilated body was found by federal investigators in March 1979 in the apartment of Ira Einhorn, stuffed in a trunk in a closet. A well-known New Age leader, Einhorn was instrumental in the late 1960s and early 1970s in promoting New Age philosophy and belief in extraterrestrial intelligences through his international network of affluent friends. He was arrested, but when granted bail skipped the country and remained one of America's most wanted men until his capture in France on June 16, 1997.

[20] Ibid., 236-238.

[21] Whitley Strieber, *Communion: A True Story* (New York: William Morrow and Company, 1987).

## Chapter Three

[1] Phil Cousineau, *UFOs: A Manual for the Millennium* (New York: Harper-Collins West, 1995), 230-247.

[2] Clark, *The UFO Files,* 62-63.

[3] Randles and Hough, *The World's Best,* 22-25.

[4] Clark, *The UFO Files,* 82-87.

[5] Howard Blum, *Out There* (New York: Pocket Books, 1990), 187-192.

[6] Randles and Hough, *The World's Best,* 26-29.

[7] Lt. Col. Charles Halt memo, January 13, 1981, photographically reproduced in *The Unopened Files,* January/February (Otley near Leeds, England: Quest Publications, 1997), 41.

[8] Jacques Vallee, *Revelations* (New York: Ballantine, 1991), 140-151.

9 Cousineau, *UFOs: A Manual*, 192-193.

10 Blum, *Out There*, 15-18.

11 *The Unopened Files*, January/February 1997, 66-69.

12 Chuck Missler, *The Return of the Nephilim* audio cassette notes (Koinonia House, PO Box D, Coeur d'Alene, ID), 3.

13 Ibid., 4.

14 *The UFO Magazine*, November/December (Otley near Leeds, England: Quest Publications 1996), 28-35.

15 *UFO Magazine*, May 1996, 9.

16 NBC "Dateline," April 19, 1996.

17 Pacheco and Blann, 111.

18 Ibid.

19 Weldon, *UFOs: What on Earth*, 85-95.

20 As cited by Weldon in *UFOs: What on Earth*, 124-127.

21 Texe Marrs, *Project Abbadon II* (audio cassette), Living Truths Ministries, 1708 Patterson Rd., Austin, TX 78733.

22 William R. Goetz, *Apocalypse Next* (Camp Hill, PA: Horizon Books, 1996), 290-291.

23 Pacheco and Blann, 118-119.

24 Budd Hopkins, *Intruders* (New York: Ballantine, 1987).

25 Ed Walters and Frances Walters, *UFO Abductions in Gulf Breeze* (New York: Avon Books, 1994). A bizarre incident connected with the Gulf Breeze sighting involved six U.S. Army intelligence specialists, just weeks before Saddam Hussein's invasion of Kuwait. The six deserted their posts in Augsberg, Germany, but inexplicably were not apprehended until five days later *in* the United States at Gulf Breeze. How they got into the country as deserters from an intelligence unit is a mystery. Vallee reports: "The six soldiers were quickly moved behind the fence at Fort Benning, Georgia, where they were interrogated by Army Intelligence, the CIA and NSA. They had left their posts, it appeared, in the burning belief that Armageddon was imminent and the rapture

prophesied by weird Christian fundamentalist sects was just around the corner and they had been designated to greet the alien spaceships at Gulf Breeze marking the return of Jesus Christ."

[26] Christopher O'Brien, *The Mysterious Valley* (New York: St. Martin's Paperbacks, 1996).

[27] Jacques Vallee, "UFO Chronicles of the Soviet Union: A Cosmic Samizdat," *The Skeptical Inquirer,* Vol. 18, No. 1/Fall 1993, 82-85.

[28] Ronald D. Story, *UFOs and the Limits of Science* (New York: William Morrow, 1981).

[29] Hynek, *The UFO Experience,* 25-26.

[30] J. Allen Hynek and Jacques Vallee, *The Edge of Reality* (Chicago: Henry Regnery Company, 1975), 45.

[31] John Ankerberg and John Weldon, *The Facts on UFOs and Other Supernatural Phenomena* (Eugene, OR: Harvest House Publishers, 1992), 7-8.

[32] Vallee, *Confrontations,* 216-218.

[33] Hynek and Vallee, *The Edge of Reality,* 23.

[34] *The UFO Magazine,* November/December 1996, 28-37.

[35] Cousineau, *UFOs: A Manual,* 230-247.

## Chapter Four

[1] The Condon Report, as quoted in Cousineau, *UFOs: A Manual,* 84.

[2] *The Bulletin of Atomic Scientists,* Fall 1967, 25-31.

[3] *OMNI Magazine,* September 1984, 63.

[4] Clark, *The UFO Files,* 52.

[5] Christopher C. French, "An Encounter with the Man from the Ministry," *Skeptical Inquirer,* January/February 1997 (Vol. 21, No. 1), 50-51.

[6] Carl Sagan, *Our Demon-Haunted World* (New York: Barnes and Noble, 1996), 267-268.

[7] Blum, *Out There*, 241-242.

[8] Ibid., 242-243.

[9] Robert Bartholomew, "The Airship Hysteria of 1896-97," *The Skeptical Inquirer*, Vol. 14, No.2/Winter 1990, 135-140.

[10] Joe Nickel and John F. Fischer, "The Crop-Circle Phenomenon: An Investigative Report," *The Skeptical Inquirer*, Vol. 16, No. 2/Winter 1992, 136-149.

[11] Fund-raising letter from The Planetary Society, Fall 1996.

[12] *Demon-Haunted World*, jacket copy.

[13] Ibid.

[14] Ibid., 75-76.

[15] Ibid., 109-110.

[16] *U.S. News and World Report*, April 14, 1997, 15.

[17] Associated Press report, *The Patriot News*, Harrisburg, PA, June 25, 1997, A2.

## Chapter Five

[1] Hugh Ross, *UFOs: The Mystery Resolved* (videotape), Trinity Broadcasting Documentary Series, available from *Reasons to Believe*, P.O. Box 5978, Pasadena, CA 91117.

[2] *UFO: The Continuing Enigma* (Readers' Digest, Pleasantville, NY: 1991), 135.

[3] Ankerberg and Weldon, *The Facts on UFOs and Other Supernatural Phenomena*, 9.

[4] Letter to the Editor, *UFO Magazine and Phenomena Report*, Vol. 12, No. 2, March/April 1997, 3.

[5] Pacheco and Blann, 381-385.

[6] John Ankerberg and John Weldon, *Spiritual Counterfeits Project Journal*, Double Issue, Vols. 1 & 2, 1992; *Alien Encounters: UFOs and the Realm of Shadows*, 26.

[7] Vallee, *Revelations*, 258-259.

[8] Ibid., 247-249.

[9] Ibid., 249.

[10] Vallee, *Dimensions*, xiv, xv, 232; *Revelations*, 217-224.

## Chapter Six

[1] Timothy Good, *Above Top Secret: The Worldwide UFO Cover-Up* (New York: Sidgewicke and Jackson, Ltd. 1987), 9.

[2] Vallee, *Dimensions,* 203, 252.

[3] Thornton Page, *UFOs and the Limits of Science* (New York: Doubleday & Company, Inc. 1976), 7.

[4] Ross, *UFOs: The Mystery Resolved.* A widely held view among ufologists and others is that there has been a long-standing government cover-up of the crash of a flying saucer at Roswell, New Mexico. It is claimed that the bodies of several aliens, as well as the crashed UFO, were recovered and are stored at a U.S. Air Force Base somewhere. One of the most convincing arguments for this theory is made by Timothy Good, a British broadcaster, in a book entitled *Above Top Secret: The Worldwide UFO Cover-Up* (New York: Sidgewicke and Jackson, Ltd., 1987). It is a well-researched, well-written volume of several hundred pages, with reproductions of numerous documents and photos made available under the Freedom of Information Act.

Nevertheless, skeptics of the Roswell story point to the virtual impossibility that the huge number of persons who would be involved in such a cover-up would be able to maintain absolute secrecy for a period of fifty *years.* The case of President Nixon's Watergate involvement is cited: A small coterie of very powerful men were unable to maintain a simple secret for more that eleven *days.*

Dr. Ross's video lecture is highly recommended viewing.

[5] Ibid.

[6] Ibid.

[7] Page, *UFOs and the Limits of Science,* 10-11.

# Chapter Seven

[1] Kurt Koch, *Christian Counseling and Occultism* (Grand Rapids, MI: Kregel Publications, 1978), 165.

[2] Dr. Koch (1913-1987), a noted German theologian, minister and evangelist, wrote over a dozen books on occultism and deliverance from demonization, most of them translated into several languages. He lectured in over 100 universities, seminaries and colleges in sixty-five countries on all five continents. His writings are marked by careful exegesis and hundreds of case histories, meticulous in their detail and accuracy.

[3] Nandor Fodor and Leslie Spence, *The Encyclopedia of Occultism and Parapsychology* (New York: University Books, 1966), v.

[4] R. Richet, *Thirty Years of Psychical Research,* as quoted by Fodor, *The Encyclopedia of Occultism,* 216-228.

[5] Ross, *UFOs: The Mystery Resolved.*

[6] Robert O. Becher, "The Relationship Between Bioelectromagnetics and Psychic Phenomena," *ASPR Newsletter,* 16 (Spring 1990): 11-14, as cited by Kenneth Ring in *The Omega Project* (New York: William Morrow and Company, Inc., 1992), 263.

[7] Kurt Wagner, "Interview with David Fetcho," in *SCP Journal,* Vol. 1, No. 2, August 1977, 20.

[8] George N.M. Tyrell, *Apparitions* (New York: Collier, 1963 rev.), chapter 2, as cited by Ankerberg and Weldon in *Facts on UFOs and Other Supernatural Phenomenon*, 31.

[9] *Angels: Friends in High Places* (Camp Hill, PA: Horizon Books, 1997), a book written by a personal friend, Rev. Jerry Orthner, explores the biblical phenomenon and doctrine of angels. The book includes the account of forty individuals who have had angelic encounters and help.

[10] Philip K. Dick, personal letters as cited by Vallee in *Revelations*, 293-294.

[11] See Ankerberg and Weldon, *Facts on UFOs and Other Supernatural Phenomena*, 38-41.

[12] Pacheco and Blann, 259.

[13] *The Cerealogist,* Summer 1995, No. 14, as cited in *The Fortean Times,* March 1997, No. 96, 36-37.

## Chapter Eight

[1] Brooks Alexander, "Machines Made of Shadows: Beyond the 'Reality' of UFOs," *SCP Journal,* 17:1-2, 11.

[2] Lynne Catoe, *UFOs and Related Subjects: An Annotated Bibliography* (Washington, DC: U.S. Government Printing Office, 1969), prepared under Air Force Office of Scientific Research Project Order 67-0002 and 68-0003, iv.

[3] John Keel, *UFOs: Operation Trojan Horse* (New York: Putnams, 1970), 299.

[4] Ross, *UFOs: The Mystery Resolved.*

[5] Ankerberg and Weldon, *Facts on UFOs and Other Supernatural Phenomena,* 44.

[6] David Hunt, "The Cult Explosion" (tract), n.p., 1981.

[7] Pierre Guerin, "Thirty Years After Kenneth Arnold," *Flying Saucer Review,* Volume 25, No. 1, p. 13, as cited in *SCP Journal,* Vols. 17:1-2, 1992, 22.

[8] Stuart Goldman, as cited in Ankerberg and Weldon, *Facts on UFOs,* 25.

[9] Patrick Huyghe, "UFO Update: The Devil's Design," *OMNI,* October 1994, 101.

[10] Ibid.

[11] Ibid.

[12] Unidentified writer cited in *UFOs: The Continuing Enigma* (Pleasantville, NY: Readers' Digest Association. Inc., 1991), 69.

[13] Strieber, *Communion,* 25-26, 181, 183.

14 David M. Jacobs, "Abductions and the ET Hypothesis," MUFON, 1988 International Symposium Proceedings: Abductions and the ET Hypothesis, 87.

15 K. Neill Foster, *Discernment, the Powers and Spirit-Speaking* (unpublished doctoral dissertation, Fuller Theological Seminary, Pasadena, CA, June 1988).

16 Ibid., 24-27.

17 Michael Miley, "The Inner Dimensions of Alien Encounter," *UFO Magazine and Phenomena Report,* Vol. 12, No.2, March/April 1997, 29.

18 Budd Hopkins, *Missing Time* (New York: Ballantine, 1988), 238-241.

19 Readers Digest, *UFOs: The Continuing Enigma* (Pleasantville, NY: The Reader's Digest Association, Inc. 1991), 84.

20 "Remind me one more time," *The Economist,* January 18, 1997, 75-77.

21 Pacheco and Blann, 356.

22 Ibid., 237.

23 Miley, "The Inner Dimensions," 29-31.

24 See John Ankerberg and John Weldon's *The Facts on Near-Death Experiences: What Does the Bible Say?* (Eugene, OR: Harvest House Publishers, 1996).

25 Vallee, *Confrontations,* 15.

26 Medicine Grizzlybear Lake, "A Native American Prophecy: A Great Purification and Earth Changes?—The UFO Contact" (*Alternative Perceptions*, Box 9972, Memphis, TN 38190), 10-15.

27 A re-reading of this book, the 1978 *UFO Missionaries Extraordinary* (New York: Pocket Books, 1975), in the light of the mass suicide, is fascinating and reveals a high degree of demonic involvement.

28 Heaven's Gate section based on 1997 reports in *USA Today*, March 27, 28, 31; *Washington Post,* March 29; *The Pa-*

*triot News*, Harrisburg, PA, March 28, 29, 30, 31; *TIME*, April 7; *U.S. News and World Report*, April 7; and *WORLD*, April 7.

[29] Weldon, *UFOs: What on Earth*, 93.

[30] *The Patriot News*, Harrisburg, PA, April 2, 1997, A8.

[31] Brad Steiger, *The Fellowship* (New York: Ivy Books, 1988), 67-68.

[32] Ruth Montgomery, *Aliens Among Us* (New York: Fawcett Crest, 1985), 2.

[33] Ibid., 10-20.

[34] Ibid., 143.

[35] Ibid., 25.

[36] Ibid., 225.

[37] Strieber, *Communion*, 216. It is instructive to realize that the title was apparently dictated by a demon. Strieber describes how it happened: "One night in April she [his wife Anne] talked in her sleep. I had thought to call this book *Body Terror* because of the extreme physical sensation of fear I had felt on December 26. Suddenly she said in a strange basso profundo voice: 'The book must not frighten people. You should call it *Communion*, because that's what it's about.' I looked over at her intending to say why I thought my title was better, and saw that she was totally asleep. Then I realized where I have heard that voice before." [It was the voice of one of Strieber's "visitors."]

[38] Whitley Strieber, *Breakthrough: The Next Step* (New York: Harper Collins, 1995), jacket copy.

[39] Ibid. In certain Masonic initiations the pattern of three knocks is significant, and in Mozart's Masonic opera *The Magic Flute* it is the indication of a move from a lower to a higher level of existence. The concept of three groups of three is also present in the Tibetan Buddhist tradition where it refers to progress in past, present and future time. Strieber

relates this to the "ancient notion of the three-in-one—positive, negative and blending forces," being the basis of the universe. The idea, related to this, of blending good and evil as seen in various Eastern religions and in entertainment like *Star Wars*, is unquestionably anti-Christian and demonic.

40 Ibid., 23, 29-33.

41 Ibid., 197, 178, 179, 204, 205, 212, 216.

42 Phil Klass as cited by William Alnor, *UFOs in the New Age* (Grand Rapids, MI: Baker Book House, 1993), 104.

43 Alnor, 29-30.

44 Pacheco and Blann, 114-115.

45 Ibid.

46 Personal interview with Dr. Walter Martin in February 1968.

47 Strieber, *Breakthrough*, 6.

48 Ankerberg and Weldon, *Facts on UFOs,* 29.

49 Hugh Ross, audio cassette of seminar lecture on ufos.

50 Keith Bailey, *Strange Gods* (unpublished manuscript), 19, 35.

51 Ibid., 21-22.

52 Weldon, *UFOs: What on Earth*, 112.

53 *Newsweek,* November 13, 1967, 38.

54 McCandlish Phillips, *The Bible, the Supernatural and the Jews* (Camp Hill, PA: Horizon Books, 1995 [reprint]). An award-winning investigative journalist with *The New York Times*, Phillips describes, in his carefully documented fashion, how an attempt was made in the 1920s to introduce America to a Hindu theosophist reputed to be indwelt by the "World Teacher." The Theosophists, whose movement appeared to be on the ascendancy, had a vision to introduce to the West not merely a new occult religion, but a new civili-

zation. According to Phillips the effort failed completely because of the Christian and spiritual climate. He writes: "Note
that Krisnamurti [the celebrated Hindu vehicle of the World
Teacher spirit] complained of *bad atmospheric conditions* pre-
vailing in the United States. Those conditions rendered him
helpless to show the supernatural effects that, in other na-
tions, had seemed to confirm his mission, both to his followers and to himself. The atmosphere in America was not, at
that time, conducive to evil spirits of the East. Upon enter-
ing the United States he was cut off from the spirits who had
produced those effects in some of his public appearances"
(p. 232). Phillips wrote in 1970 and at that time convincingly presented his argument that the spiritual climate in
America had deteriorated to the point that, in contrast to
what happened in the '20s, the continent was now quite defenseless against an occult invasion: "Since the mid-1960s,
North America has come under massive invasion by evil
spirits. The attack is especially concentrated on youth.
Though people see the results of it, they are at a loss to explain the destructive forces" (p. 112).

55 "$125,000 to Guerillas," *The Globe and Mail*, Toronto,
September 22, 1981, A3, citing reports in a major magazine
and a network TV news program.

56 Francis Schaeffer, *Whatever Happened to the Human Race?*
(Old Tappan, NJ: Fleming H. Revell, 1979), 21.

57 Brad Steiger, "UFO Contactees: Heralds of the New Age"
*UFO Universe*, Summer 1989, No. 6.

58 Bailey, *Strange Gods*, 35-36.

59 John Mack, *Abduction: Human Encounters with Aliens*
(New York: Charles Scribner's Sons, 1994), 32.

60 Vallee, *Revelations*, 134.

# Chapter Nine

1 See John Mack, *Abduction: Human Encounters with Aliens*
(New York: Charles Scribner's Sons, 1994).

2 Whitley Strieber, *Catmagic* (New York: Tom Doherty Associates, Inc., Books, 1986), v.

3 Whitley Strieber, as quoted by William Alnor in *UFOs in the New Age* (Grand Rapids, MI: Baker Book House, 1993), 105.

4 Karla Turner, *Into the Fringe: A True Story of Alien Abduction* (New York: A Berkley Book, 1992), introduction.

5 C.B.D. Bryan, *Alien Abduction, UFOs and the Conference at M.I.T.* (New York: Alfred A. Knopf, 1995).

6 Christopher O'Brien, *The Mysterious Valley* (New York: St. Martin's Paperbacks, 1996).

7 Edith Fiore, *Encounters: Case Studies of Extraterrestrial Abductions* (New York: Ballantine, 1989).

8 Phillips, *The Bible, the Supernatural and the Jews*, 245-267.

9 Ibid., 213.

10 Ibid., 211.

11 Ibid., 308-309.

12 *TIME*, February 21, 1997, 43.

13 *American Family Association* Newsletter, March 30, 1997, 1.

14 Ibid.

15 Kenneth Miller, "Star-Struck," *LIFE*, July 1997, 39-53.

16 *Publishers' Weekly*, May 18, 1997, 19.

17 Susan Bauer, "Stephen King's tragic kingdom," *Books and Culture*, March/April 1997 (Vol. 3, No. 2), 14-15 as cited in *Current Thoughts and Trends* (newsletter), May 1997.

18 Douglas Groothuis, "Technoshaminism: digital deities in cyberspace," *Christian Research Journal*, Winter 1997 (Volume 19, Number 3), 37-43, as quoted in *Current Thoughts and Trends*, July 1997, 5-6.

19 Ed Murphy, *The Handbook for Spiritual Warfare* (Nashville, TN: Thomas Nelson, 1992), 6-8.

[20] Phillips, *The Bible, the Supernatural and the Jews*, 206-225.

[21] Foster, *Discernment, the Powers and Spirit-Speaking*, 179-217.

[22] G. Ferguson, as quoted by Foster, 148.

[23] Kurt Koch, as cited by Foster, 191.

[24] Erica Goode, "The eternal quest for a new age." *U.S. News and World Report*, April 7, 1997, 32-34.

[25] Richard Lacayo, "The lure of the cults," *TIME*, April 7, 1997, 45-46.

## Chapter Ten

[1] Barry Downing, *The Bible and Flying Saucers* (New York: Berkley, 1989).

[2] *Spiritual Counterfeits Project Journal*, 17:1-2, 43.

[3] Weldon, *UFOs: What on Earth*, 165.

[4] Walter Martin as cited in *UFOs in the New Age* (Grand Rapids, MI: Baker Book House, 1993), 227.

[5] Weldon, *UFOs: What on Earth*, 164.

[6] Murphy, *Handbook for Spiritual Warfare*, 557.

[7] Ibid., 22.

[8] Adapted from a *Reasons to Believe* position paper, n.a., n.d.

[9] Strieber, *Communion*, 35, 274, 108, 172, as quoted by Ankerberg and Weldon, *Facts on UFOs*, 22-23.

## Chapter Eleven

[1] See *Evidence That Demands a Verdict* (San Bernardino, CA: Campus Crusade for Christ, 1972), *More Evidence That Demands a Verdict* (San Bernardino, CA: Campus Crusade for Christ, 1975), and *More Than a Carpenter* (Wheaton, IL: Tyndale, 1978)—all by Josh McDowell.

## Chapter Twelve

[1] Foster, *Discernment, the Powers and Spirit-Speaking*, 231.

# Appendix A

1 *Secret Vows: Our Lives with Extraterrestrials* (New York: Berkley Books, 1995) is the extremely bizarre, purportedly true story by Bert and Denise Twiggs, who claim to have intermarried with an extraterrestrial couple and to have had fifteen children between them! Another far-out example is the offer by a British insurance broker (Goodfellow Rebecca Ingrams Rearson) to insure against impregnation by extraterrestrials, as reported by *The Toronto Sun*, August 27, 1996. Weird!

2 Hugh Ross, "Sons of God . . . Who Are They?" (position paper, n.d.), available from Reasons to Believe, P.O. Box 5978, Pasadena, CA 91117.

3 Chuck Missler, "Return of the Nephilim," *Koinonia House*, P.O. Box D, Coeur d'Alene, ID.

4 Arnold Clinton, *Powers of Darkness* (Downers Grove, IL: InterVarsity Press, 1992), 66.

5 I.D.E. Thomas, *The Omega Conspiracy* (Herndon, VA: Growth, 1986), 104.

6 Clifford Wilson, *The Chariots Still Crash* (New York: Signet, 1976), 152-153.

7 J. Sidlow Baxter, *Studies in Problem Texts* (Grand Rapids, MI: Zondervan, 1960), 152.

8 Gleason Archer, *Encyclopedia of Bible Difficulties* (Grand Rapids, MI: Zondervan, 1982), 80.

9 Ibid., 79.

10 Hank Hanegraaff, "Questions and Answers," *Christian Research Newsletter*, Vol. 9, Issue 3, Fall 1996, 4-5.

# Appendix B

1 Julia Ingram and G.W. Hardin, *The Messengers* (Lake Oswego, OR: Skywin, 1996), 67-68.

2 Ibid., 180.

[3] Ibid., 181.

[4] Ibid.

[5] Ibid., 170.

[6] Ibid., 215.

# BIBLIOGRAPHY

Note: A listing in this bibliography does not imply approval of the contents or conclusions of a book. It is merely a partial list of the materials used in the research.

"Alien Encounters: UFOs and the Realm of Shadows" *Spiritual Counterfeits Project Journal*, Vol. 17:10-2, 1992.

Alnor, William M. *UFOs in the New Age*. Grand Rapids, MI: Baker, 1993.

*Alternate Perceptions, A Journal of UFOs, History, Native Spirituality and Paranormal Phenomena*, Issue #37, Winter 1997.

Anderson, Neil. *The Bondage Breaker*. Eugene, OR: Harvest House, 1990, 1993.

_____. *Victory over the Darkness*. Ventura, CA: Regal, 1990.

Ankerberg, John and Weldon, John. *The Facts on UFOs and Other Supernatural Phenomena*. Eugene, OR: Harvest House, 1992.

Arnold, Clinton. *Powers of Darkness*. Downers Grove, IL: InterVarsity, 1992.

Berlitz, Charles and Moore, William. *The Roswell Incident*. New York: Berkley, 1988.

Blum, Howard. *Out There*. New York: Pocket Books, 1990.

Bryan, C.B.D. *Alien Abduction, UFOs and the Conference at M.I.T.* New York: Alfred A. Knopf, 1995.

Bubeck, Mark. *The Adversary*. Chicago: Moody, 1975.

Clark, Jerome. *The UFO Files*. Lincolnwood, IL: Public International, 1986.

Cousineau, Phil. *UFOs: A Manual for the Millennium*. New York: Harper Collins West, 1995.

Crystal, Ellen. *Silent Invasion*. New York: St. Martin's, 1991.

*The Devil's Advocate*, Issue #7, Box 10853, Pensacola, FL 32524.

Dione, R.L. *God Drives a Flying Saucer*. New York: Bantam, 1993.

Drake, W. Raymond. *Gods and Spacemen in the Ancient East*. New York: Signet, 1968.

Edwards, Frank. *Flying Saucers, Serious Business*. New York: Bantam, 1966.

Fiore, Edith. *Encounters*. New York: Ballantine, 1989.

Foster, K. Neill. *Discernment, the Powers and Spirit-Speaking*. Unpublished doctoral dissertation, Fuller Theological Seminary, June 1988.

Friesen, James G. *Uncovering the Mystery of MPD*. Arrowhead Springs, CA: Here's Life, 1991.

Fuller, John G. *Incident at Exeter*. New York: Berkley Medallion, 1966.

_____. *The Interrupted Journey*. New York: Berkley Medallion, 1966.

*The Gate, Explore the Mysteries,* Volume Three, Issue Twelve, January 1997. P.O. Box 43516, Richmond Heights, OH 44143.

Geller, Uri and Playfair, G.L. *The Geller Effect*. New York: Ballantine, 1986.

Good, Timothy. *Above Top Secret: The Worldwide UFO Cover-up*. New York: Sidgewicke and Jackson, 1987.

_____, ed. *Alien Update*. New York: Avon, 1992.

Greenwood, Barry, J. *Clear Intent: The Government Cover-up of the UFO Experience*. Englewood Cliffs, NJ: Prentice-Hall, 1984.

Hewer, Hayden and Steiger, Brad. *UFO Missionaries Extraordinary*. New York: 1976.

Hilstrom, Elizabeth L. *Testing the Spirits*. Downers Grove, IL: InterVarsity, 1995.

Hopkins, Budd. *Intruders*. New York: Ballantine, 1987.

_____. *Missing Time*. New York: Ballantine, 1988.

Hynek, J. Allen. *The UFO Experience: A Scientific Inquiry*. Chicago: Henry Regnery, 1972.

Ingram, Julia and Hardin, G.W. *The Messengers*. Lake Oswego, OR: Skywin, 1996.

Jung, C.G. *Flying Saucers*. New York: MJF Books, 1978.

Keel, John A. *The Mothman Prophecies*. New York: Illuminet, 1991.

Koch, Kurt. *Christian Counseling and Occultism*. Grand Rapids, MI: Kregel, 1978.

_____. *The Occult ABC*. Grand Rapids, MI: Kregel, 1986.

Lansberg, Alan and Sally. *The Outer Space Connection*. New York: Bantam, 1975.

Larson, Bob. *UFOs and the Alien Agenda*. Nashville: Thomas Nelson, 1997.

Lewis, David Allen and Shreckhise, Robert. *UFO: End-Time Delusion*. Green Forest, AK: New Leaf, 1993.

Lore, Gordon I.R., Jr. and Deneault, Harold H., Jr. *Mysteries of the Skies: UFOs in Perspective*. London: Prentice-Hall, 1968.

Mack, John E. *Abduction: Human Encounters with Aliens*. New York: Charles Scribner's Sons, 1994.

Mandelker, Scott. *From Elsewhere: Being ET in America*. New York: Dell, 1995.

Marrs, Texe. Two-volume set of audio tapes *Project Abbadon I & II*, 1996.

Martin, Walter M. *UFOs: Friend, Foe or Fantasy* (audio tape). Christian Research Institute, 1965.

MacMillan, John A. *The Authority of the Believer*. Camp Hill, PA: Christian Publications, 1997.

Menzel, Donald H. and Taves, Earnest H. *The UFO Enigma*. Garden City, NY: Doubleday, 1977.

Michaels, Susan. *Sightings*. New York: Simon & Schuster, 1996.

Montgomery, Ruth. *Aliens Among Us*. New York: Fawcett Crest, 1985.

Murphy, Ed. *The Handbook for Spiritual Warfare*. Nashville: Thomas Nelson, 1992.

O'Brien, Christopher. *The Mysterious Valley*. New York: St. Martin's, 1996.

Pacheco, Nelson S. and Blann, Tommy R. *Unmasking the Enemy*. Arlington, VA: Benden, 1994.

Penn-Lewis, Jessie. *War on the Saints*. New York: Lowe, 1993 (reprint).

Phillips, McCandlish. *The Bible, the Supernatural and the Jews*. Camp Hill, PA: Horizon Books, 1995.

Randle, Kevin D. *A History of UFO Crashes*. New York: Avon, 1995.

Randle, Kevin D. and Schmitt, Donald R. *The Truth About the UFO Crash at Roswell*. New York: M. Evans and Company, 1994.

Randles, Jenny. *UFOs and How to See Them*. New York: Sterling, 1992.

Randles, Jenny and Hough, Peter A. *World's Best "True" UFO Stories*. New York: Sterling, 1994.

Readers' Digest Association, ed. *UFO: The Continuing Enigma*. Pleasantville, NY: Readers' Digest, 1991.

Ring, Kenneth. *The Omega Project*. New York: William Morrow, 1992.

Ripp, Bobby. *End Time Deceptions*. Mandeville, LA: True Light Ministries, 1996.

Ross, Hugh. *UFOs: The Mystery Resolved* (videotape), 1995. Available from Reasons to Relieve, P.O. Box 5978, Pasadena, CA 91117.

"The Roswell File" (cover story). *TIME*, June 23, 1997, pp. 62-71.

Sagan, Carl. *Our Demon-Haunted World*. New York: Random House, 1995.

Sagan, Carl and Page, Thornton. *UFOs: A Scientific Debate*. New York: Barnes and Noble, 1996.

*The Skeptical Inquirer*, Vol. 14, No. 2/Winter 1990. "The Airship Hysteria of 1896-97," pp. 171-181; "New Evidence of MJ-12 Hoax," pp. 135-140.

_____, Vol. 16, No.2/Winter 1992. "Crop Circles: Hype, Hoaxes, and Hoopla," pp. 136-149.

_____, Vol. 16, No. 3/Spring 1992. "The Avro VZ-9 'Flying Saucer'," pp. 287-291.

_____, Vol. 16, No. 4/Summer 1992. "Follow-Up: UFO Crash?," pp. 428-29.

_____, Vol. 17, No. 2/Winter 1993. "The Big Sur 'UFO': An *Identified* Flying Object," pp. 180-187.

_____, Vol. 17, No. 2/Winter 1993. "David M. Jacobs, *Secret Life: Firsthand Accounts of UFO Abductions*," pp. 197-200.

_____, Vol. 17, No. 3/Spring 1993. "Have UFO-Abductions and Near-Death Experiences a Common Origin?," pp. 315-316.

_____, Vol. 18, No.1/Fall 1993. "Diagnoses of Alien Kidnappings That Result from Conjunction Effects in Memory," pp. 50-51; "UFO 'Dogfight' in Kentucky," pp. 3-4; "Alien Stigmata, Shy Craft, and a UFO Conference," pp. 21-23, and "Jacques Vallee, *UFO Chronicles of the Soviet Union*," pp. 82-85.

_____, Vol. 18, No. 2/Winter 1994. "Round in Circles: Physicists, Poltergeists, Pranksters and the Secret History of Cropwatchers," pp. 191-194.

_____, Vol. 19, No. 1, Jan/Feb 1995. "Air Force Report on the Roswell Incident," pp. 41-48.

_____, Vol. 19, No. 3, May/June 1995. "Crop Circle Mania Wanes," pp. 41-43.

_____, Vol. 19, No. 4, July/Aug 1995. "The Roswell Incident and Project Mogul," pp. 15-18.

_____, Vol. 19, No. 6, Nov/Dec 1995. " 'Alien Autopsy' Show-and-Tell," pp. 15-16; " 'Alien Autopsy' Hoax" pp. 17-19, and "The GAO Roswell Report and Congressman Schiff," pp. 20-22.

_____, Vol. 20, No. 3, May/June 1996. "A Study of Fantasy Proneness in the Thirteen Cases of Alleged Encounters in John Mack's *Abduction*," pp. 18-20.

_____, Vol. 20, No. 6, Nov/Dec 1996. "That's Entertainment: TV's UFO Cover-up," pp. 29-31.

_____, Vol. 21, No. 1, Jan/Feb 1997. "Open Skies, Closed Minds: For the First Time a Government UFO Expert Speaks Out," pp. 50-53.

Smith, Warren. *The Book of Encounters*. New York: Zebra Books, 1976.

Steiger, Brad. *The Fellowship*. New York: Ivy Books, 1988.

_____, ed. *Project Blue Book*. New York: Ballantine, 1990.

Stemman, Roy. *Visitors from Outer Space*. Garden City, NY: Doubleday, 1976.

Story, Ronald D. *UFOs and the Limits of Science*. New York: William Morrow, 1981.

Strieber, Whitley. *Breakthrough: The Next Step*. New York: Harper Collins, 1995.

_____. *Communion*. New York: William Morrow, 1987.

_____. *Transformation*. New York: Avon, 1988.

Stringfield, Leonard H. *Situation Red*. Garden City, NY: William Morrow, 1977.

Sullivan, Walter. *We Are Not Alone*. New York: Signet, 1964.

Sutherly, Curt. *Strange Encounters*. St. Paul, MN: Llewellyn, 1996.

Time-Life, ed. *The UFO Phenomenon*. Alexandria, VA: Time-Life, 1987.

_____. *Alien Encounters*. Alexandria, VA: Time-Life, 1992.

Turner, Karla. *Into the Fringe: A True Story of Alien Abduction*. New York: A Berkley Book, 1992.

Twiggs, Denise Rieb and Twiggs, Bert. *Secret Vows: Our Lives with Extraterrestrials*. New York: Berkley, 1995.

Tyson, Basil. *UFOs: Satanic Terror*. Beaverlodge, Alberta: Horizon House, 1977.

*UFO Magazine*, November/December 1996.

_____, January/February 1997.

*UFOs: The Hidden Truth* (video). New Liberty Films and Videos, n.d.

*Unexplained UFO Mysteries*. Publication of Weekly World News, Boone, IA, October 8, 1996.

Unger, Merrill. *What Demons Can Do to Saints*. Chicago: Moody, 1991.

Vallee, Jacques. *Anatomy of a Phenomenon: UFOs in Space*. New York: Ballantine, 1965.

_____. *Confrontations*. New York: Ballantine, 1990.

_____. *Dimensions*. New York: Ballantine, 1988.

_____. *Messengers of Deception: UFO Contacts and Cults*. Berkeley, CA: Andor, 1979.

_____. *Passport to Magonia*. Chicago: Contemporary Books, 1993.

_____. *Revelations*. New York: Ballantine, 1991.

_____, and Vallee, Janine. *Challenge to Science: The UFO Enigma*. New York: Ballantine, 1966.

Von Daniken, Eric. *Chariots of the Gods*. New York: Bantam, 1974.

_____. *Gods from Outer Space*. New York: Bantam, 1975.

Walters, Ed and Walters, Frances. *UFO Abductions in Gulf Breeze*. New York: Avon, 1994.

Weldon, John with Levitt, Zola. *UFOs: What on Earth is Happening?* New York: Bantam, 1976.

# Index

## A

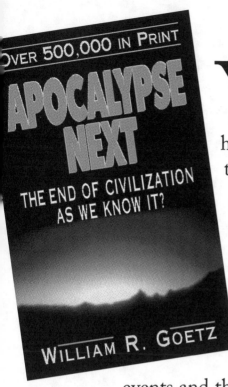